THE WORLD OF
MACAWS

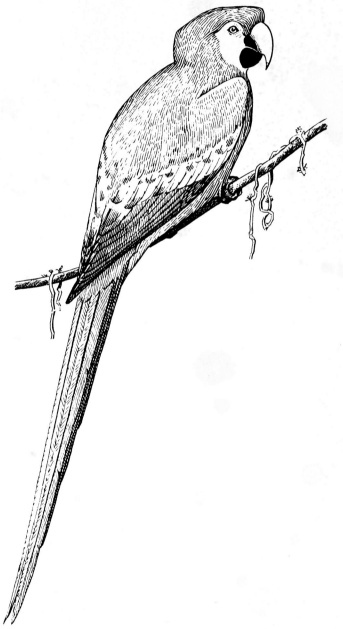

Dieter Hoppe

translated by Arthur Freud and R. Edward Ugarte

Illustrations: Thomas Arndt, 61-3, 61-4, 89-6, 93-3, 125-5. Glen S. Axelrod, 81, 89-5, 124-1. Dr. Herbert R. Axelrod, 17, 25-2, 25-3, 89-4. Horst Bielfeld, 28-1, 53-2. Isabelle Francais, 24-1, 29, 89-3. F. Gorski, 21-3. Wolfgang de Grahl, 125-6. Dieter Hoppe, 20-2, 21-1, 21-2, 24-2, 28-2, 28-4, 52-1, 53-4, 56, 57-2, 57-3, 85-1, 85-2, 93-2, 93-4, 93-5, 93-6, 96-1, 96-3, 116-3, 117-1, 117-2, 117-3, 117-4, 117-5, 117-6, 120-2, 121, 124-2, 124-3, 125-1, 125-2, 125-4. Ralph Kaehler, 120-1, 124-5. H. Leibfarth, 57-4. A. F. Lydon, 49, 64, 113, 128. Horst Müller, 57-1, 92. H. Reinhard, 28-3, 53-1, 116-1, 116-2. Paul Roth, 20-1, 21-4, 25-4, 52-2, 52-3. Dr. U. Schürer, 124-4. Tony Silva, 21-5, 53-3. Louise Van der Meid, 32-3, 96-2. Franz Veser, 84. Franz Veser/Dieter Hoppe, 32-1, 32-2. M. L. Wenner, 25-1. G. Wilking, 117-7, 120-3, 125-3.

Distributed in the UNITED STATES by T.F.H. Publications, Inc., 211 West Sylvania Avenue, Neptune City, NJ 07753; in CANADA by H & L Pet Supplies Inc., 27 Kingston Crescent, Kitchener, Ontario N2B 2T6; Rolf C. Hagen Ltd., 3225 Sartelon Street, Montreal 382 Quebec; in ENGLAND by T.F.H. Publications Limited, 4 Kier Park, Ascot, Berkshire SL5 7DS; in AUSTRALIA AND THE SOUTH PACIFIC by T.F.H. (Australia) Pty. Ltd., Box 149, Brookvale 2100 N.S.W., Australia; in NEW ZEALAND by Ross Haines & Son, Ltd., 18 Monmouth Street, Grey Lynn, Auckland 2 New Zealand; in SINGAPORE AND MALAYSIA by MPH Distributors (S) Pte., Ltd., 601 Sims Drive, #03/07/21, Singapore 1438; in the PHILIPPINES by Bio-Research, 5 Lippay Street, San Lorenzo Village, Makati Rizal; in SOUTH AFRICA by Multipet Pty. Ltd., 30 Turners Avenue, Durban 4001. Published by T.F.H. Publications Inc. Manufactured in the United States of America by T.F.H. Publications, Inc.

Contents

Preface

Parrots, a group of birds consisting of 328 species, have in the past two centuries won the hearts of many bird lovers. Their cheerful activity, their high intelligence, their facility for learning to speak, their ability to be easily tamed, and, last but not least, their incredible richness of color have induced many people to become more closely involved with these feathered acrobats.

Macaws, the quintessential parrots, are probably the most striking and best-known representatives of their kind. Every bird lover and bird breeder secretly cherishes the wish to own such an animal. Macaws are very intelligent and sensitive birds. Therefore, every fancier who intends to own and care for such a house pet should thoroughly acquaint himself in advance with the nature of these birds. And so should the experienced breeder, because successful macaw breeding is possible only when the birds are offered conditions which correspond as closely as possible to the conditions of their life in the wild. This book about macaws gives information about all the criteria for keeping them and should serve the serious bird lover as a basic guide.

The decline of wild animal populations—and of parrots in particular—in many cases is currently both menacing and alarming. For the fancier and keeper of psittacine birds there is necessarily an obligation to work to the limit in order to successfully breed those birds now in captivity. Their future presence in the hands of fanciers will certainly depend on regularly successful captive breeding, as we cannot count indefinitely on the importation of wild parrots in the wake of species-protection treaties.

I am grateful to Dr. Joachim Steinbacher of Bad Homburg and Dr. Claus König of the Museum of Natural History in Stuttgart for scientific source material and for their advice regarding taxonomic problems. Many thanks are also due the fanciers and the breeders, my coworkers at zoological gardens and natural-history museums, and also my correspondents in South America who have helped me with many particular problems through their advice and valuable suggestions. I am especially grateful to the publishers, Eugen Ulmer Verlag of Stuttgart, who with this volume about macaws in their series on exotic cagebirds have ventured to make a comprehensive presentation of this interesting group available to parrot fanciers.

DIETER HOPPE

Esslingen, Spring 1983

4

Parrots and Mankind

The first live parrots were brought to Europe by Onesicritos, the helmsman of Alexander the Great (356–323 B.C.), and probably were one of the species of the genus *Psittacula*. Thus, three hundred years before our era, the first parrots were described in Greece. Aristotle (384–322 B.C.) comments on the "crooked-clawed" birds, and by this he means parrots: "All birds with crooked claws have a short neck and a wide tongue, and they are mimics. Such a one is the Indian bird *Psittake*, which is said to be human tongued. He gets drunk when he drinks wine." Later on, the Romans rapidly raised the keeping of parrots to a veritable cult. The birds occupied places of honor in elegant homes, were instructed by specially appointed teachers, and were kept in the most expensive cages made of silver, ivory, and tortoise shell. Unfortunately, ancient Rome carried matters to excess: Emperor Heliogabalus served his guests a dinner with parrot and peacock heads on silver dishes and, in addition, tossed live parrots to his lions for a meal.

In the Middle Ages, through the Crusades and expanding trade routes, the first parrots arrived in Central Europe. Frederick II (1212–1250), the grandson of the Emperor Barbarossa, owned a White Cockatoo (*Cacatua alba*), which he had received as a thank-you gift from the Sultan of Babylon. His dissertation on falconry was the first Western book about birds. Frederick II's experiments and observations were based on scientific principles; thus, for example, he had an incubator built in order to hatch eggs and to be able to observe the development of the chicks.

The Spanish and Portuguese (and later the English, French, and Dutch), who in the fifteenth and sixteenth centuries were trying to conquer Central and South America and the surrounding islands, discovered parrots of incredible magnificence of color among the natives. Parrots were kept as a living source of food and feathers not only by the primitive tribes but also by the highly developed Indian cultures. Mayan and Aztec noblemen adorned themselves with the iridescent feathers of macaws (*Ara*) and the Resplendent Quetzal (*Pharomachrus mocinno*). The Spanish chronicler Diaz del Castillo, who with Cortez in 1519 traveled throughout Mexico, was very impressed by Montezuma's aviaries, in which the rarest birds were kept and bred. The quetzals that supplied the Aztec rulers with the coveted feathers were abundantly represented. If a trespasser killed a quetzal, he was sentenced to death. Soon the parrots collected by the Spaniards arrived on European soil, and here they became showpieces in the houses of kings and princes.

The great thirst for knowledge at that time, as well as the constant discovery of new animal and plant species, enabled sciences which dealt in detail with the new and the unknown to arise. Conrad Gesner (1516–1565), a Swiss physician and naturalist as well as a universal scholar and bibliographer, created as his life's work the *Historia Animalum* in five volumes, a description of animal species that can be regarded as a fundamental scientific presentation, forward-looking for its time. In his work Gesner described fourteen parrots, including the Blue-and-yellow (*A. ararauna*) and Scarlet (*A. macao*) macaws. Among other things about the Blue-and-yellow, Gesner mentions that "in regard to the large blue-and-saffron-yellow parrots, *Psittacus maximus cyanocroceus*, his daily meals have been almonds, nuts, meat, and bread. During the day he has drunk only once and then actually only toward evening. If apples or pears have been tossed to him, he has immediately split the same with his beak, taken out the little seeds and eaten the same with the greatest enjoyment, and then has thrown the rest away."

In his notes, Gesner relies chiefly on the statements of the Italian naturalist Aldrovandi. The accurate information in the species accounts disseminated the principal observations of some living creatures still very strange in those days. In addition, the book was composed according to a system, grouping related kinds of animals together. With his two volumes about birds, Gesner laid the foundation of ornithology, and thus he may be regarded as one of its pioneers. Nevertheless, nearly two hundred years had to elapse before ornithology was recognized as a branch of science.

Ornithology, the study of birds, thus began as a side branch of zoology. Parrots, though both their provenance and their relationships to other orders of birds were hardly understood at that point in time, were especially interesting to many scientists. Persons such as Dr. Johann Latham (1740–1837), Johannes Baptist von Spix (1781–1826), William Swainson (1789–1855), and Carolus Linnaeus (1707–1778), and others must not be disregarded when one studies the beginnings of parrot research.

The rise in popularity of parrots began in the last century, when these feathered acrobats were introduced to animal lovers on a wide scale in zoological gardens. At the time, the tropical romanticism of the Central European population, constantly excited by new reports of discoveries from these distant countries, aroused a desire for the exotic, the unknown, and the strange. Parrots embodied this exotica in their appearance, their behavior, and their provenance, and consequently, even in those days it was a short trip from their tropical homelands to the living rooms of city folk.

Prof. Dr. Friedrick O. Finsch (1839–1917), a highly respected ethnologist and ornithologist of his time, instructed bird lovers with his volume on parrots (1867–1868), giving detailed comments on species and provenance, as well as on the cage-keeping and care, of hookbills. Many other authors emulated Finsch. The continual discovery of new species and races—as well as their importation, first to England, Holland, and Germany—contributed to the fact that every newly published bird book was already outdated upon appearance.

Dr. Karl Russ described 230 species in his handbook for bird fanciers, which appeared in 1870. In the second edition, he treated 700 species. The fourth edition, which was published in the year 1900, contained over 900 species. In the edition of Russ's handbook that was revised by Karl Neunzig in 1920, there are 1450 species of birds described in detail, including a large number of the parrot species known today. The following was reported at that time about the rare Glaucous Macaw (*Anodorhynchus glaucus*):

Blue Macaw—*Ara glauca* (Vieill.). Seablue Macaw—Engl., Glaucous Macaw. Males and females gray blue; head and feathered lores grayer, tinged with brown on the cheeks, throat, and upper breast; the rest of the underside becoming somewhat greenish; inner vanes of the wings and tail feathers, as well as the underside, and the greater under wing coverts brownish black, while the lesser are greenish gray blue; the eye is dark brown; the naked area around the eye and the base of the lower mandible yellow; beak and feet blackish. Length, 650–750 mm; wings 350–360 mm; tail, 375 mm. Range: southern Brazil, Paraguay, Uruguay; said to nest in riverbank cavities and in holes in trees; inhabitants of virgin forests. Rare, although now and then found in the trade; first kept in the zoological garden in London, then in the zoological garden in Berlin since 1892; food, etc., the same as other macaws.

In the third edition of another book by Dr. Karl Russ, *Die sprechenden Papageien,* which appeared at Magdeburg in 1898, we find the following concerning the Glaucous Macaw:

The Seablue Arara (*Psittacus sittace-glaucus,* Vll.). Blue Macaw—Glauceous Macaw—*Ara bleuâtre*—*Grijsblauwe Ara.*

Almost rarer than the aforementioned; also like it in all characteristics, or at least very similar; it is dusky seablue; head, cheeks, and throat more grayish or greenish blue; wings and tail feathers black brown on the inner vanes, brown black beneath; lesser under wing coverts light seablue; beak black; eyes dark brown; feet blackish brown; size significantly less than that of the Hyacinth-blue Macaw (Length, 72.8 cm.; wing, 33.8–36.5 cm.; longest tail feather, 33.8–36.5 cm.). Range: southern Brazil, Paraguay, and Uruguay. In 1860, one was sent to the zoological garden of London; others came to the zoo at Amsterdam in 1868 and to Berlin Zoo in 1892. Some have been present in exhibits and in bird stores recently. As previously, the price for freshly imported specimens was 350 marks.

The quotations from these books reveal how high the level of knowledge of these exotic animals was at that point in time.

The illustrations in a small Viennese parrot book (see Günther 1957), made from the original watercolors of the natural-history collection belonging to Ferdinand I of Austria, clearly depicted the various species. In addition, the book contained instructions on maintenance and gave information about the characteristics of parrots. About the Cuban Macaw (*Ara tricolor*), already rare at that time and which now, unfortunately, is included among the extinct species, the book reports the following:

Three-colored Macaw — Yellow-naped Arara — Tricolored Macaw — *Ara tricolore* — *Driekleur Ara* — *Psittacus tricolor* Behst.

This macaw is one of the smaller species. It attains only pigeon size and is native to the island of Cuba, where it is said to have already become truly rare. It is seldom seen in captivity, so it is a true stroke of luck that it was preserved for us here in a picture by L. Brunner. Its darker scarlet red, together with the dark orange-colored occiput, nape, and upper back, clearly distinguishes it from the other reddish macaws. The eye is yellow, the feet horn brown. The tail is copper red with the end-third blue, and the entire underside is likewise dark red. This is a bird that one will hardly ever see in pictures, let alone see alive.

Not only did bird fanciers show great interest; famous ornithologists at the museums of natural history were also attracted by the incredible variety of forms in this exotic group of birds. Men like Hans Carl Hermann Ludwig, Count von Berlepsch (1850–1915), Dr. Alfred Edmund Brehm (1829–1884), Prof. Dr. Friedrich Otto Finsch (1839–1917), Dr. Ernest Johann Otto Hartert (1859–1933), and Prof. Dr. Anton Reichenow (1847–1941) — to name just a few German scientists of the period — contributed to the research on these species. Obscure people explored the remotest, most uninhabitable corners of the earth: Henry Walter Bates spent eleven years of his life, from 1848 to 1859, in the lowlands of the Amazon River and collected 14,000 animal species there, of which 8000 were completely unknown to science. The evaluation of their "booty" made the systematic classification of animal forms and the cataloguing of species and races possible.

The great demand for parrots could scarcely be satisfied. Of the larger species, the genera *Amazona*, *Ara*, and *Psittacus* were preferred; of the smaller, *Melopsittacus* and *Agapornis*. Adventurers throughout the world specialized in catching them, and seamen who traveled to countries overseas brought these parrots back with them and sold the animals to supplement their meager wages. Consequently, the harbor cities became ports of entry for animals of all kinds. Soon stores that specialized exclusively in the buying and selling of animals sprang up. Other merchants and small businesses supplied the necessary equipment, such as cages and food dishes, and soon a new "branch" of the economy had grown. Often, the business of selling living creatures was conducted under the most bizarre conditions. The spread of psittacosis was the result of these abuses. In 1934, a law was passed [in Germany] which forbade the importation of parrots for reasons of health generally, and directives were issued in order to eliminate the conditions for psittacosis infection completely. Forty years passed before this law was rescinded. Today, fanciers can again delight in caring for and breeding parrots, and by close observation of the birds they can also contribute important details to scientific ornithology.

Evolutionary History

The evolutionary history of birds is not unequivocally verifiable because of their delicate bone structure and its consequently swift decomposition. Birds can, however, be traced back with certainty to *Archaeopteryx*, of which a fossil was found in the year 1861 in a fine Jurassic limestone deposit in Solenhofen slate. *Archaeopteryx* was followed in Upper Jurassic by the genera *Ichthyornis* and *Hesperornis*; though *Ichthyornis* was already a good flyer, both still had reptilian teeth (a toothed upper jaw). The evolution of birds probably can be traced back along some other branch of the evolutionary tree, like that of the mammals; apparently their precursors were arboreal reptiles. By close to sixty million years ago birds should have lost completely the reptilian characteristics persisting in them and assumed their final, present-day form. From this stage of their development date the orders known to us today; in the course of evolution these were followed by families, subfamilies, genera, species, and subspecies.

The existence of parrots can be traced back to the Oligocene (the third epoch of the Tertiary Period), forty to fifty million years ago. Fossils of parrots from this epoch have been found in France, and detailed research has revealed a close relationship to the Grey Parrot (*Psittacus erithacus*). The origin of parrots should by no means be sought in Europe. They probably originated in the area of northern Australia and New Guinea; thus, this region should be viewed as the primal home of parrots. Because parrots occupy almost a special position in the class of birds and few ancestral relationships with other families of birds can be recognized, their development cannot be traced completely. Pesquet's Parrot (*Psittrichas fulgidus*), which still survives today, and the Nestorinae too exhibit an ancient appearance and may certainly be regarded as primitive parrots. The Kakapo (*Strigops habroptilus*), another primitive form which lives in New Zealand, either has been separated from the evolutionary course for many millions of years or has developed from another primitive form and thus should be regarded as a connecting link to this already extinct ancestor of the parrots. This bird has many distinctive characteristics: the inability to fly (only gliding flight over a short distance is possible); the bones are almost without air chambers; the feathers around the beak are bristly like those of owls; and indigestible cellulose fibers ingested with the food are regurgitated in pellet form. Furthermore, the Kakapo is a purely ground-dwelling, nocturnal bird that breeds in two-year cycles. Even the inflatable throat pouch differentiates it markedly from its so-called relatives.

As was already mentioned, the origin of parrots is to be sought in the area of New Guinea and northern Australia. From these areas an unbelievable variety of species developed. Today we know of 328 species of parrots, with the most diverse characteristics. In parrots the first and fourth toes point backward and serve for grasping and climbing. The upper mandible has a joint of its own and can be moved upward. The tongue is quite thick and muscular and has some taste and touch papillae (in lories the tongue is brushlike). The tail feathers consist of six pairs (*Oreopsittacus* is an exception). Nearly all parrots have evolved into cavity nesters; thus, one finds parrot nests in tree cavities, holes in the earth, and rock crevices. An exception is the Monk Parakeet (*Myiopsitta monachos*); it is a colony nester which builds gigantic nest structures out of twigs fashioned to form a sort of cavity.

The variations in size among the groups of parrots are quite remarkable; the smallest, the Buff-faced Pygmy-Parrot (*Micropsitta pusio*), attains a size of only 8.5 cm.; the largest, the Hyacinth Macaw (*Anodorhynchus hyacinthinus*), can grow to be 100 cm. long. Their incredible color variations range from a monochromatic dark gray to dazzling color combinations that attain impressive splendor. These plumages, in the course of thousands of years, were developed by the birds as adaptations to their world.

Macaws in the Wild

Distribution. The four macaw genera, which include seventeen living species, are restricted to Middle and South America, except for some that inhabit islands off the coast. The most northerly extension of the environment suited to macaws is occupied by the Military Macaw (*Ara militaris mexicana*), which is found up to 27° north latitude in southeastern Sonora and southwestern Chihuahua in Mexico. To the south, macaws have occurred as far as northwestern Uruguay.

Very few other parrot species exceed the range of the macaws to the north or south. Today, macaws are not represented on the islands of the Caribbean Sea, with the exception of Trinidad. The last evidence of a macaw from the Caribbean area dates from 1885 and mentions at the same time the date of its extinction—the reference is to the Cuban Macaw (*Ara tricolor*). The occurrence of macaws was reported in previous centuries from other islands of the Greater and Lesser Antilles, although documented proof of the presence of these species was never produced. Some macaw species have tremendous ranges; thus, for example, the range of the Scarlet Macaw extends from central Mexico (Oaxaca) almost continuously southward to Santa Cruz in Bolivia. Thus, the area inhabited by Scarlet Macaws extends along a zone running from northwest to southeast for a stretch of more than 6600 km. Likewise, the Blue-and-yellow Macaw (*Ara ararauna*) and the Red-and-green Macaw (*Ara chloroptera*) occupy huge areas on the South American land mass. But other macaw species occur in biotopes very limited spatially. The Blue-headed Macaw (*Ara couloni*), an extremely rare species of its genus, is found only in a small area of eastern Peru. The Red-fronted Macaw (*Ara rubrogenys*) has an even more limited habitat in central Bolivia.

It may be assumed that the population size of a species is comparable to the extent of its range; i.e., those species that occupy small amounts of surface area are much smaller in numbers than those macaws which settle over a wider range. The following mathematical example should clarify this point: Blue-and-yellow Macaws are distributed over at most 10 million km² of the South American continent, which has a total area of about 17.8 million km². If one realizes that 40% of these 10 million km² is fully usable habitat for the macaws, then the actual range is 4 million km² in size. The Red-fronted Macaw lives in a zone approximately 10 thousand km² in size. However, the actual area available to the use of the birds, after subtracting the regions inhabited by people as well as those which cannot serve as habitat for the birds, amounts to about 25% of the range area and is therefore about 2500 km². If one compares the effective size of the Blue-and-yellow Macaw's range with the actual habitat of the Red-fronted Macaw— 40 million to 25 hundred km²—then mathematically the ratio becomes 16,000:1; this means that for every 16,000 Blue-and-yellow Macaws there is one Red-fronted Macaw.

R. S. Ridgely (1980) estimates that the range of the Red-fronted Macaw is about 50 x 100 km in size, and he believes that the wild population has been reduced to 3000 animals at most. This example may serve as a rule of thumb, though the situations of endangered species are not taken into consideration.

Macaws are very gregarious animals which, except for the incubation and nestling periods, congregate in flocks of a hundred or more animals. A social hierarchy such as one sees in the primates or various mammalian groups is not evident with macaws or other parrot species. There are no "ring-leaders" directing the flock; nor are there any "sentries" to guard feeding and sleeping places. The macaw flock is a unit in which all birds hold equal positions. Dominance is noticeable only in the relationship between males and females (as pairs), whereby the males are dominant for a large part of the year. At breeding time and especially while the young are being reared, in nearly all species of the four genera there is a reversal of the social hierarchy.

Macaws, with their wide, extensive distribution, populate the tropical and subtropical zones and are found in areas up to 1000 m. above sea level. The Military Macaw (*Ara militaris*) is found in Mexico even at altitudes up to 2500 m. where a moderate climate prevails. The birds prefer to stay in hilly areas along rivers. Large expanses of virgin lowland forest are used by macaws only seldom, or in passing. They avoid the widespread mature virgin forest, but otherwise they are found in all other landscapes of the subtropical and tropical zones. The thornbush plains of the chaco, the canyonlike dry river valleys of the caatinga, the flood plains of Paraguay, the great mangrove swamps near the coast, and the semiarid regions of the Mexican highland valleys—all are habitats suited to the birds. An almost constant supply of food, except in the southernmost and northernmost parts of their range, means that the macaws are rarely compelled to wander locally to any great extent. One can definitely characterize the animals as sedentary birds, since macaws in their daily flights traverse an area about 40 x 40 km. (1600 km²), returning to their point of departure, their sleeping places, at some time in the evening. Rarely have flights over greater distances been confirmed. Detailed research of a few macaw flocks over a long period of time confirmed that the birds systematically harvested the food-bearing trees in the vicinity of their sleeping place. At the moment that the food supply is exhausted, their residence is shifted to the next adjoining area.

Way of Life. The macaw species prefer various kinds of palm nuts as their principal food. Many of the hard-shelled nuts can be opened and eaten only by the larger species. Macaws, in contrast to other bird species or species related to them, enjoy the advantage that when the fruit is ripe, these trees can be harvested only by them, as other birds and animals are not in a position to crack open these hard nuts. The habit of eating palm fruits gives the macaws a remarkable extra advantage in comparison to smaller parrots. As is well known, the fruits of the palm hang from the upper part of the 30-meter-high trunks. The various predatory birds and

reptiles that specialize in catching birds cannot reach these areas. The long, smooth palm trunks also offer fine protection against enemies. Of course, palm nuts are not the only food eaten by macaws. All the wild fruits and berries, as well as leaf and flower buds, also serve as food, so that one can consider the food eaten by the macaws to be varied and rich in nutrients.

The course of the day, in fact the entire course of a macaw's life, is very structured and goes according to plan. As was mentioned before, except for the incubation and nestling periods, the animals combine into groups, so that the smaller species often form flocks with over a hundred members. In the evening, parties fly to the so-called "sleeping trees," mostly large trees that have died off, in which the flock spends the night. The trees which have been chosen by macaws for roosting emerge above the adjacent vegetation, as a rule, or stand isolated in swampy areas or in clearings, and therefore offer a certain protection from natural enemies. Thus, for example, a sneak attack by predatory animals or birds is immediately detected by the parrots, and enough time remains for flight. The quarreling for the best sleeping places often produces a deafening noise that frequently lasts for hours after nightfall. Shortly after sunrise, the assembled flock breaks up, and small groups fly off to the feeding places. These diurnal assemblages, which in the larger species consist of at most four to twenty animals (the smaller macaws more often form larger groups), as a rule are maintained all day. The ripe food trees are visited on the same flight route daily, with the birds flying around intervening highlands. The flights between the sleeping and feeding places are undertaken at heights of 60–80 m. above the ground. Over short stretches, the macaws fly at low altitudes above the trees. In flight these birds are extremely impressive. The slim body, the long tail which tapers rearward, and the large wing span present a magnificent sight. With slow beats of their wings (which basically are not raised above the body) and by direct flight, the animals attain considerable speed. During flight, contact calls are voiced constantly, which probably have the purpose of keeping the birds together. Bonded pairs fly very close to one another, so that their wings are practically touching. After landing in the food trees, the birds eat copiously, behaving

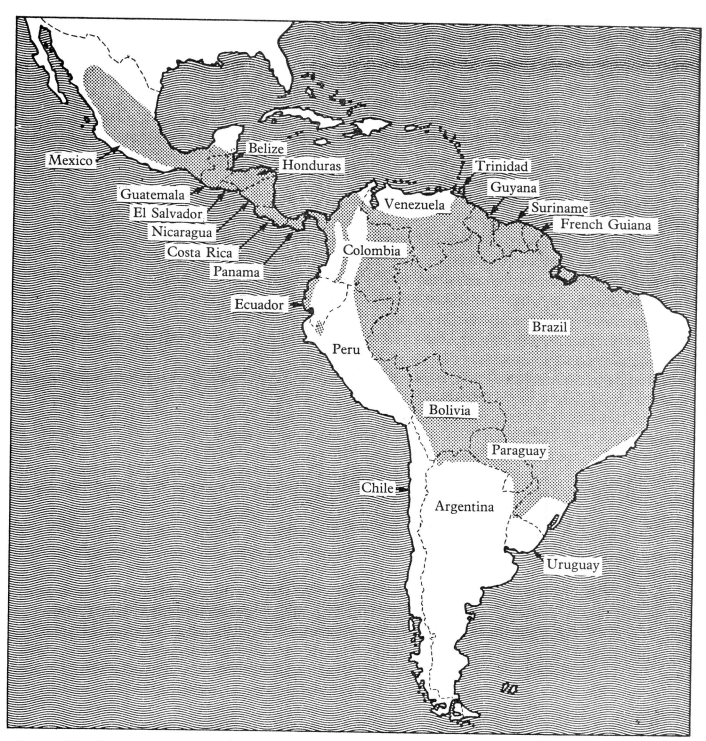

Range of the four genera of macaws.

very calmly. Only falling hulls, remnants of food, and droppings reveal their presence. In the wild, macaws maintain very great fleeing distances from people; therefore, it is difficult to approach them. This may also be the reason why the animals very rarely venture onto plantations; also, cultivated fruit is only a supplementary food, of secondary importance to them. During the hot midday hours macaws rest and devote themselves mainly to preening their feathers. Later in the afternoon the return flight to the sleeping trees begins. Occasionally but regularly, the birds visit sloping banks to eat the clayey loam, which contains minerals and salts.

Sexual maturity probably takes place during the fifth year, with the smaller species of macaws maturing two years earlier. The author has kept many macaws through the years and thus has noticed that three-year-old Blue-and-yellow Macaws courted, exhibiting the same behavior as adult birds. The possibility definitely exists that macaws are already sexually mature in their early years. Only breedings in fanciers' aviaries can elucidate this; the evidence cannot be acquired by observation in the wild.

How the macaws achieve pair bonding and by what criteria the birds choose their mates is not known. One can be certain that subadult, sexually immature birds, are already inclined to pair off. Like many other large parrots, macaws also practice monogamy for life; i.e., changing mates probably never occurs. It should be noted that the observations and references to the lifelong monogamy of these birds refer purely and simply to animals held in captivity; from this evidence it is simply assumed that animals living in the wild behave just like those in captivity. Thus, this proposition about monogamy for life cannot be scientifically proven up to this point, and it is questionable whether it can ever be established unequivocally.

In the southernmost part of their range, macaws reproduce sometime after the beginning of October. To the north this starting point is postponed until the following months. In Guyana and Panama the courting season occurs in January and February, and in Mexico it may be observed from March or April. The beginning of the breeding season is closely linked to the rainy season; hence, one can conclude that rain is an effective agent in inducing breeding. The sexually mature pairs that belong together separate from the flock and devote themselves to searching for a suitable nesting site. It is not clear to what extent macaws return to nesting sites used in previous years or whether new ones are sought out annually. Since the large macaw species need spacious cavities for rearing their young, suitable nesting places are, for the most part, found only in large trees or dead palms, which with their smooth trunks also offer good protection from climbing enemies. For the smaller species the search for nesting sites is simpler, because there are by far many more suitable places for nesting available to them. Almost everywhere macaws occur, their breeding season overlaps that of other bird species that nest in cavities, so that frequently nesting places must be defended against competitors. Many nests of eggs or fledglings fall victim to this competition.

A long period of time elapses between courtship and the young chicks becoming fully self-sufficient, especially in the larger macaw species. One can assume that courtship and searching for a nesting site take about four weeks. From the laying of the first egg to the hatching of the young takes another thirty days, since tight incubation does not always occur with the first egg laid. The nestling period can take up to 110 days. After leaving the nest, the offspring are still fed by the parent birds for at least thirty days. Shortly afterwards, all rejoin the flock, but for a time the family unit can still be recognized, either because they perch close together or fly near one another. Courtship behavior as well as rearing the young will be treated more fully in the accounts of the various species.

In their extensive range, macaws have a host of natural enemies. They give special attention to constantly observing their surroundings. Outstanding vision enables the animals to discern enemies at a great distance and to take the necessary measures to protect themselves. For the most part this amounts to flight, accompanied by deafening screams. The principle enemies of the macaws are the Harpy Eagle (*Harpia harpyja*) and the Ornate Hawk-Eagle (*Spizaetus ornatus*). These species of birds of prey inhabit an area which extends from southern Mexico to northern Argentina, almost coextensive with the range of the macaws. Both species of raptors repeatedly find their prey among the macaws. Even the huge Hyacinth Macaw with its powerful beak cannot defend itself against these predators. In the Aripuanã region in northernmost Mato Grosso, P. Roth repeatedly observed that Orange-breasted Falcons (*Falco deiroleucus*), which are substantially smaller than the large macaws, would attack Blue-and-yellow and Scarlet macaws. This falcon is a good hunter on the wing and preys on flying macaws. For the most part, the macaws can evade the falcon by flying fast as an arrow toward the ground shortly before they are intercepted. Once on the ground or in the trees, they can successfully defend themselves, so the falcon immediately breaks off its attack.

Environmental Changes Threaten the Macaws.
The principal danger to the macaws, however, is environmental change brought about by man. In the past twenty years a third of the Amazon forest has been sold for commercial purposes. The constant demand by European and North American industrialized nations for commercial timber and decorative lumber led to this unthinkable exploitation of nature. For example, years ago the Brazilian government surrendered the lumbering rights to the underdeveloped northeast to a North American concern. Using bulldozers as much as possible, the rainforest is converted into fine furniture or newspapers for the interests and prosperity of the firm. A paper factory erected in the same location provides for easy transport of the wood products. Meanwhile, it is well known that tropical forest land, after being cleared, is agriculturally useful for only three years at best and then becomes completely barren; yet immense forest areas are still being cut clean to the ground. Tropical downpours hasten the process of erosion and in a very short time wash away the extremely shallow layers of humus. The ground dries out, and the vegetation assumes a scrubby, often steppelike, character.

A further example can demonstrate the dire future environmental threats to animal and plant life in the virgin Amazon forest of Peru. The Peruvian national oil company, Petroperu, has signed a thirty-year agreement with Shell, the British-Dutch oil concern, to open up oil fields in the Amazon region. The government in Lima has granted Shell the rights to develop an area of two million hectares (20,000 km²) in the Peruvian part of the Amazon basin. Shell, in turn, must pledge to invest at least $100 million in the next six years to open up the region.

It is commendable when, for the good of the country, agreements are concluded which will ensure the long-term future of the affected populace and provide economic stability to the state. Of course, the conflict inherent in such agreements soon becomes apparent. For example, Brazil in past years lost vast expanses of virgin forest through commercial exploitation, so that the Brazilian government found itself forced to take the control of the development of the country into its own hands in order not to entrust it completely to foreign firms, for whom only short-term profits count.

In Peru the virgin forests of the Amazon were still in a pristine condition a few years ago. But after oil was discovered, huge bulldozers ate into the green wilderness and destroyed the forest. Today the drilling towers shoot out of ground and overshadow the green canopies of the virgin-forest giants, and the swamps are pumped full of oil for fear of snakes. Indigenous animal and plant species are driven out or destroyed. The ecosystem that took millennia to develop may be thrown completely out of balance in a few months and changed in such a manner that the effects are still not nowadays understood. Like all animal species, the macaws are also driven from habitat developed over millennia. The constant environmental changes caused by the expansion of agricultural and industrial zones and the extensive lumbering in the virgin forests of Middle and South America (Brazil lost almost its entire stand of *Araucaria* forest in its southern provinces) contributed just as much to the obliteration of the original forest as the quest for oil, gold, silver, diamonds, iron, copper, tin, titanium, lead, uranium, nickel, bauxite, coal, etc. If thoughtful consideration and appropriate action to preserve nature is not taken in the years to come, then it is likely that the ecosystem in the area will be thrown completely off the track. Fortunately, already taking hold in some countries of the Third World at this time is an attitude whereby one gradually reflects on the biological order and ecological balance and tries to avoid the mistakes of the past.

The Washington Convention (CITES). On March 3, 1973, a treaty was signed in Washington to regulate international trade in wild fauna and flora. In this way, species which are in danger of extinction are protected in a practical way through a trade embargo, and species which are threatened by commerce can be involved in trade only with an official permit. Up to now, more than sixty-five countries have become parties to this agreement. The Bundestag of the Federal Republic of Germany, with ratification by the Bundesrat, passed the law to become a signatory to the Washington Convention in May 22, 1975. The announcement of the law appeared on May 28, 1975, in the *Bundesgesetzblatt*, Nr. 35, Seite 773–883.

The nations party to the Washington Convention have compiled the following communiqué as a preamble to the regulations:

RECOGNIZING that the fauna and flora living in the wild constitute in their beauty and complexity an irreplaceable component of the natural system of the earth, it behooves us to protect them for present and future generations;
ACKNOWLEDGING that the significance of wild fauna and flora constantly increases in esthetic, scientific, and cultural terms, and in respect to health and the economy as well;
RECOGNIZING that peoples and nations can protect their wild fauna and flora best, and that they should protect them;
RECOGNIZING that the international cooperative effort for the protection of designated species of wild fauna and flora from excessive exploitation by international trade is vitally important;
ACKNOWLEDGING the necessity to take appropriate measures without delay . . .

Articles I to XXV of the treaty provide definitions of categories. In the Appendices I to III, species which face extinction, species which are threatened, and species worth protecting are enumerated. In Appendix I of the Washington Convention, the species especially in danger of extinction are listed. In order to guarantee the survival of these species— which in many instances already seems extremely doubtful—traffic in specimens is prohibited. Exceptions can be made by the appropriate authorities for a special permit when appropriate; such special permits are not granted for cases where personal gain is involved.

It is interesting for the macaw fancier to note that the Glaucous Macaw (*Anodorhynchus glaucus*), Lear's Macaw (Anodorhynchus leari), and Spix's Macaw (*Cyanopsitta spixii*) are listed in Appendix I of the Washington Convention. The author subscribes to the opinion that Appendix I should be immediately expanded to include the Hyacinth Macaw (*Anodorhynchus hyacinthinus*), the Red-fronted Macaw (*Ara rubrogenys*), and the Blue-throated Macaw (*Ara glaucogularis*). With the other macaw species, especially Great Green and Military macaws (*Ara ambigua* and *Ara militaris*), trade must be very strictly controlled by establishing an annual quota of birds that may be captured for export.

The species mentioned in Appendix II of the Washington Convention can be marketed only under the condition that in every case the government-designated scientific authority of the exporting country has issued an export permit. An export permit can be issued only if the following conditions can be met:
(*a*) If the scientific authority of the exporting country has announced that this export is not detrimental to the survival of the species.
(*b*) If the executive authority of the exporting country has confirmed that the specimen has not been obtained through violation of the legal prescriptions promulgated by the country for the protection of animals and plants.
(*c*) If the executive authority of the exporting country has confirmed that every living specimen will be prepared for transport and dispatched so that the danger of injury, damage to health, and animal suffering will be eliminated as much as possible.
Importation into the Federal Republic of Germany is thus possible only when the exporting country fulfills the above mentioned conditions (*a*) through (*c*).

After the third conference of the signatories to the Washington Convention (which met from February 25 through March 8, 1981, in New Delhi) additions were made to Appendices I and II, and the Federal Republic of Germany reported no reservations. Since June 6, 1981, these amendments have been in effect in their entirety for the Federal Republic of Germany. In New Delhi it was decided, among other things, to add to Appendix I three additional amazon-parrot species (*Amazona arausiaca, A.*

barbadensis, and *A. brasiliensis*), Coxen's Double-eyed Fig-Parrot (*Cyclopsitta diophtalma coxeni*), and both races of the Thick-billed Parrot (*Rhynchopsitta pachyryncha*). It was further agreed to place all the parrot species, except those already mentioned in Appendix I, on Appendix II of the Washington Convention. The only exceptions are the Cockatiel (*Nymphicus hollandicus*), the Rose-ringed Parakeet (*Psittacula krameri*), and the Budgerigar (*Melopsittacus undulatus*). For these three species, Appendix III of the Washington Convention is applicable. This new resolution binds the treaty nations to supervision of one hundred percent of the parrot trade. Should the scientific authorities of the exporting nations confirm that commerce involving one species or another becomes harmful to the species, they can cut off trade at any time.

The regulation of commerce in parrots by Appendices I and II of the Washington Convention is a welcome precaution; however, the menace of habitat destruction, the root of the entire problem, is not considered. In the opinion of the author, the threat to species originates first and foremost with the destruction and exploitation of the natural environment. Day after day, mankind sacrifices vast biotopes and thereby destroys the biocoenosis, the living community of animals and plants. Even now, very few parrot species are in a position to adjust to the environmental changes wrought by man. Therefore, the consideration arises as to whether it is possible for animals and plants that no longer have any chance of surviving in the wild to at least be preserved in very small numbers.

From the point of view of the parrot fancier, this is an instance: The wild population of the Puerto Rican Amazon (*Amazona vittata*) was estimated in 1968 to be fifteen to twenty animals. An assistance program with a permanent staff was formed for the preservation of the species, even though from a genetic point of view it seems questionable whether survival is possible at all. A program was developed under the best possible conditions in the Luquillo National Forest Reserve, the last refuge of the Puerto Rican Amazon. So far, the success achieved has been small: the stock has been increased to fifty. One fears that if the program were ended, habitat conditions would be so altered that the Puerto Rican Amazon would have no chance of survival. It would be only a few years until the last ones were gone. In this case it is easy to understand how changes in the natural environment brought about by mankind can be responsible for the extinction of one animal species; it will be the same with other parrot species. Why don't we consider putting the last wild Puerto Rican Amazons into the care of experienced parrot breeders? There are many breeders or associations of breeders which would be in a position, through appropriate accommodations and care suitable to the species, to preserve these birds by means of successful breeding. In this way, the stock could probably be increased enough to make subsequent reintroduction possible. Lovers of nature and animals must look on with sadness and disillusionment as more and more ecosystems, the foundations of our lives, which took millennia to develop, are being sacrificed within a very short time for so-called progress. What is the sense of laws, such as the Washington Convention for the protection of species, which regulate commerce in threatened species but fail to prevent the destruction of the natural environment?

Care and Breeding

Buying a Macaw. Careful consideration combined with a bit of self-evaluation should precede the decision to take on a house pet. It should be clearly understood that when one acquires a living creature, this changes the subsequent course of its life or, in any case, at least influences it very strongly. One should also obtain detailed information from local club members or animal keepers prior to the proposed purchase of an animal, in order to learn further details about maintenance. Likewise, one should also keep in mind that during every vacation trip, or even a weekend excursion, someone must always look after the animal left behind. Thus, the projected animal purchase must be discussed in detail with all the family members concerned. Only when one has thoroughly weighed all the "ifs and buts" and still decides to acquire a parrot, should he proceed to buy one.

Of the large family of parrots, macaws are especially recommended as pets, since with the proper accommodations they can become quite lovable household companions. Prior to the purchase of the bird, a place for the cage must be selected. A well-lit spot near a window is best. Since macaws come in very different sizes (the smallest is about 30 cm. long and the largest attains a length of almost 100 cm.), a suitable cage is important.

Although macaws are considered typical parrots, their ability to talk is not nearly as pronounced as, for example, that of the amazons (*Amazona*) or the Grey Parrot (*Psittacus erithacus*), which is an artist at talking and mimicking. But a few macaw species do have a definite talent for learning to talk. There are isolated cases of animals which are markedly gifted talkers and learn whole sentences, but these are exceptional.

Among the larger macaws, the Scarlet Macaws (*Ara macao*) make very lovable house pets, as do the Blue-and-yellow Macaws (*Ara ararauna*) and the Red-and-green Macaws (*Ara chloroptera*). Among the smaller macaws, the Chestnut-fronted Macaws

(*Ara severa*), the Yellow-collared Macaws (*Ara auricollis*), Illiger's Macaw (*Ara maracana*), and the Red-shouldered Macaw (*Diopsittaca nobilis*) are good pets. All the species mentioned rapidly become tame as youngsters and show talent for imitating words, whistles, and noises. The author is of the opinion that a bird's gift for talking can be remarkable and often even funny, but should never be the sole reason for acquiring a macaw. Other considerations are more important; a very significant criterion is how personable one group of animals or another is.

Large parrots have very rarely been raised in captivity. Only in the past few years have several breeders, who made great efforts to breed macaws, seen their attempts succeed. It is very encouraging that these efforts are being vigorously continued. Nevertheless, the buyer will find it difficult to purchase a domestically raised macaw in Germany; therefore, it is suggested that you buy from an authorized animal dealer. The animals for sale in the trade have by law been medicated during quarantine; therefore, it is advisable to observe the animals over a long period of time before deciding to buy. When buying, one should heed the following suggestions. Watch the animals on display over a long period of time. Notice how the bird reacts when you approach the cage. A macaw should not sit apathetically, but, should you examine it more closely and if it is not yet tame, it should retreat and maintain fleeing distance. Make sure that the bird breathes normally, has no nasal discharge, and that the eyes are not tearing and there is no indication of watery droppings.

Young macaws may be recognized by their irises, which as a rule are brownish. Of course, the change in iris color can take quite a variable amount of time. In the accounts of the different species, the coloration of young animals is gone into in detail. Should the iris color have already reached its final stage, then one should note the bird's beak and feet. A young macaw has a smooth beak and only

Attempts to rear the Red-bellied Macaw (*Ara manilata*) have been successful only recently and on a small scale.

slightly scaly feet. It is not possible to determine age from the color of the plumage.

Take notice of which foods the bird you choose is being fed. If the bird is accustomed to being fed abundantly with various seeds, nuts, and fruits, it will continue to expect them. Also, it is difficult to convert a macaw that eats only sunflower seed to other kinds of food. A one-sided diet for the bird causes deficiencies to appear and leads to diseases, with frequently fatal results. Slightly damaged plumage or clipped wing feathers should not be an impediment to the sale, because with the next molt these feathers will be shed and replaced by new ones. On the other hand, missing claws do not grow back. Macaws which have lost claws through biting or injuries are only potentially able to breed, since the animals cannot stand sufficiently steady for copulation.

Every breeder and importer of parrots [in Germany] is required by law to band the animals and to register the banding. The macaw you acquire must be banded. If there is no leg band, one must suppose that the bird was brought into Germany illegally or comes from an unauthorized breeder. Do not be surprised if the seller of a parrot asks you for your name and address. He is obligated to be able to provide information about persons to whom he sold his birds. Thus, in the event of an outbreak of a contagious disease, the trail of the parrot can be traced and the disease fought.

After purchasing the macaw, it should be brought to its new quarters in the shortest possible time. Where long distances are involved, use a suitable shipping box, one that has a securely mounted perch. For trips that take a long time, food and water should be at the bird's disposal.

Accommodations. Because of their huge size and their powerful beaks, macaws, except the few small species, require especially spacious and solidly constructed aviaries and cages. Structures made of insufficiently rigid metal will hold up to their beaks for only a few days, while those made of wood are not suitable at all. When buying or building a suitable cage, a few points are worth noting.

The larger macaws when seated are one meter long; this means that a cage that measures at least 100 x 100 cm. in area and 170 cm. in total height is necessary. Shops generally carry a small assortment of large cages, but only a few of these are actually suitable. It is absolutely necessary that the wire mesh be quite strong. The vertical and horizontal wiring should be at least 3 mm. thick, and the points at which they are welded should not be more than 10 cm apart. If they are farther apart, it will be possible for the birds to bend the wire with their beaks until the welds break. This causes the entire structure to lose its solidity, and in a few days it will become weak and flexible. Highly recommended are sturdy spot-welded mesh and wavy mesh with a mesh size of about 50 x 50 or 50 x 100 mm. The ends of the wire must be welded to a steel frame running horizontally and vertically. The cage door should be quite large, so that after opening the door every corner of the cage can be reached by hand. It is ideal if the entire front of the cage is made to be a door. This makes it very easy to clean the cage, and the perching arrangements can be modified or renovated without difficulty. Furthermore, the macaw can then easily leave its cage to enjoy some freedom. Food bowls and drinking utensils should be situated at perch height, and they should be solidly mounted in such a manner that they cannot be moved or tipped over by the birds. It is advisable to have for the cage floor a tray which can be easily removed and cleaned. Tree branches of various thicknesses are the best perches, but the thinnest branches should still be large enough that they cannot be encircled by the bird's toes.

A cage of the size mentioned is not the only accommodation needed for a macaw. A solid cage will serve during the acclimation period and for sleeping quarters for the macaw, but, of course, the bird should not be kept solely in the cage. In the summer, one should provide an open perch on the terrace or in the garden. A Christmas-tree stand or other support to hold a tree branch, set on a large tray, perhaps with casters, will serve the purpose nicely. A stirrup-shaped perch may also be fastened to the ceiling.

The ideal place to keep a macaw is an outdoor flight with a shelter room attached. This offers the birds the greatest possible opportunity to flourish; they can spend all day from spring through fall in the fresh air, taking full advantage of the sun and rain. Aviary planning must be done carefully, so that the many details are taken into account.

Detailed instructions for building an aviary are readily available. It is important to lay out the flights according to a definite plan, employing a kind of modular scheme. Mesh partitions to divide the flight section should be easily removable by hand, so that the birds can be kept together in a group except during courtship, incubation, and breeding. That the entire flight section must be massively constructed of masonry, steel frames, and galvanized iron mesh is self-evident. For large structures, one should also plan on a water supply, a heating system, a humidifier, and eventually running water and light-dimming facilities. It is also advisable to provide a kitchen area with a freezer and a small stove.

Acclimation and Care. Keeping macaws is in no way more of a problem than keeping species similar to them. However, the decision to acquire and keep an animal will decisively influence the manner and course of your life. A living creature must be cared for constantly, and this does not mean only five days a week. One should also realize that birds kept in an apartment or home always produce a certain amount of "dirt," and, as a result, you must reach for the vacuum far more often than in a bird free dwelling. If you have weighed all of the so-called annoyances in a critical manner and discussed them with all the members of the family involved, and you still decide to buy the animal, then it can be assumed that you are starting off on the right foot.

After purchasing your macaw, bring it to its new home via the shortest route. Avoid direct contact with the bird, so that it will associate as few unpleasant experiences as possible with the human hand. Thus, one should try to get the macaw into its cage without grabbing it. This can be done without difficulty if the cage door is large enough. Obviously, the cage will have been set up in advance. Water and food dishes have been filled, and sufficient bird sand has been spread on the floor. In addition, perches—tree branches wherever possible—have been firmly anchored so that they cannot slip. After the bird has been moved into its new quarters, it should be left alone for the first few days, except for the time it takes to feed it and clean the cage. The cage should stand in a sunny, draftfree place, but not close to a radiator, because

the warm air rising from it will dry out the bird's skin and may cause irritation, which may result in feathers being chewed or plucked. In order to disturb the macaw as little as possible during the first few days of acclimation, approach the cage very cautiously and avoid quick body movements. Small children, who are often quite lively, should also be kept away from the bird for the first few days. House pets such as dogs and cats must slowly be accustomed to their new roommate.

After a few days, the macaw will familiarize itself with its new situation, become calmer, and slowly adjust to its new owner. It will soon be evident which foods the macaw shows a preference for; these tidbits can be used to make an attempt at feeding by hand. Of course the bird will be afraid of the nearness of the hand during these first feeding attempts and will retreat to the farthest corner of the cage. As time passes, however, its shyness will subside, and it will accept the proffered food with its beak, very cautiously and nervously at first. Under no circumstances should one deprive the bird of food in order to compel it to eat from your hand. Macaws can hold the larger kinds of food such as nuts or pieces of fruit firmly in their claws and bite off small pieces. They are not the only parrots which eat the larger foods this way. "Eating from the paw" always amuses bystanders; people witnessing it for the first time are always astonished. Small twigs or roots are also held tightly in the claws so they can be chewed. During climbing, the beak serves as a prehensile organ. On the ground, macaws move around awkwardly, with an extremely clumsy gait. When they are climbing among the branches, macaws are not nearly as graceful as other large parrot species, for they move carefully and slowly.

After the macaw has become familiar with its new owner and its new environment, it can then be permitted to have its first outing from its cage. Near the cage, set up a climbing tree—made of tree branches, if possible—and then open the cage door. The bird now has the opportunity to climb directly from the cage onto the climbing tree. Never compel the bird to leave the cage, for it has come to regard it as its home; the animal must decide to do so itself. If it does not attempt to climb on the tree the first time, it will certainly do so later on. Once it has learned to leave the cage on its own and to

1▲   2▼

1. Groves of buriti palms, which occur mainly in the moister areas of dry regions, serve as permanent dwelling places for many macaw species. The fruits of the palms *(Mauritia* sp.) are an important food for the larger parrots. 2. Mangrove swamps, found not only in river deltas but also the sea coast and the river courses of the interior, often cover huge areas. Many macaws choose to spend the night on such "forest islands."

The largest species in the family of parrots is the Hyacinth Macaw *(Anodorhynchus hyacinthinus)*, which may reach a length of one meter. Nothing can withstand the incredible force of their beaks. **1.** Lifting the wings is a gesture of threat. **2.** This Hyacinth Macaw pair in the Leibfarth collection soon laid eggs but, unfortunately, the clutch was not incubated. **3.** A Hyacinth Macaw in the posture of attentive observation. **4.** This photo taken in the wild by P. Roth shows the typical flight formation of bonded pairs. **5.** Hyacinth Macaw chick about 45 days old.

return, such excursions will soon become a matter of habit.

Macaws seldom fly in confined areas; therefore they cover the distance either by climbing or walking. If a place is set up for your pet on a balcony or terrace for summer days, and it can't be enclosed with a mesh screen, then it is advisable to clip the bird's wing feathers to prevent it from flying away. Under no circumstances should the macaw be kept on a leg chain; the risk of injury is too great, and freedom of movement is sharply curtailed. The author regards "chain keeping" as a form of cruelty to animals. If one keeps an exotic bird as a house pet, then he must meet all of the creature's needs and provide the best and most natural living conditions. Trimming the wing feathers is relatively simple, but it does require some basic knowledge. It is best if two people undertake the "wing clipping." One person holds the macaw, while the second person fans out the wing with one hand and with the other uses sharp scissors to cut off part of the flight feathers, about 3–4 cm. from the flesh. The outermost two feathers are left uncut, since in this way the folded wing still looks nice. It is not necessary to clip both wings. When clipping wings, it is absolutely vital to realize that only fully grown feathers are cut. Fresh feather sheaths are fed with blood and will bleed profusely if cut. The resulting wound will take a long time to heal, or under certain circumstances may never heal.

Similar caution is required when cutting the claws. Under normal conditions, cutting long claws is not necessary. If one offers his birds branches of different thicknesses as perches and replaces them every two to four weeks, the claws will be worn down and not grow too long. If the claws still become too long, then they can be shortened with a strong nail scissor or a side-clipper. Use extreme caution, because two-thirds of the claw contains a blood supply. An injury may cause the claw to grow crookedly; thus, only the extreme tip of the claw should be cut. The same is also true for the upper mandible. A macaw which is regularly supplied with fresh branches and pieces of wood will keep itself busy for hours gnawing; this way, the beak is used enough that it does not become too long. It is best to take the bird to an experienced animal dealer, breeder, or veterinarian to have the claws and beak trimmed.

Most macaws consider it a great treat to stay out in the rain on mild summer days. They ruffle their feathers and often turn somersaults, so that the water can reach every part of the body. Their cries of glee during bathing underscore their feeling of well-being. Not every bird's accommodations allow it to be put out in the rain. However, since a rain bath or shower is important for a macaw's plumage, one should spray the bird once or twice a week with a mister. The bird's shower should take place during the morning or midday hours, so that the feathers will be dry again by dusk. Not every macaw is enthusiastic about a soaking; there are many animals which derive no pleasure at all from a shower and try to avoid getting wet. However, if a macaw does not care for a bath, it should still be sprayed regularly, at least once a week, as this artificial rain washes the dust from the plumage.

Macaws love companionship. In the wild they often devote hours to mutual feather care. Thus, the feathers, especially in the mate's head and neck regions, are preened, and the new feathers, which emerge from the skin in sheaths, are opened. It is difficult for the sheaths to open without outside assistance; therefore, a macaw kept singly should be given help in the care of its feathers. If the bird is tame, it will repeatedly come to its human and hold out its head to be scratched. One should then open the new feather sheaths at the tips, which are not supplied with blood. The tame macaw will allow this assistance with the greatest pleasure.

In time a macaw kept in the house will become a "family member" and take part in all activities, but love for the animal should not be carried to excess.

Some macaws are inclined to feather mutilation: the birds chew their own feathers. In some extreme cases, feather eating progresses so far that all the feathers are plucked from those body regions that can be reached with the beak. This bad habit is most common in macaws kept singly in the home. At present it is not possible to fully explain the cause of feather eating or plucking. Several unfortunate circumstances seem to drive the birds to this kind of self-mutilation. One significant contributing factor in feather eating may be found in the fact that most animals in captivity languish for want of a suitable mate. Other circumstances such as vitamin and mineral deficiences, boredom, lack of humidity, or improper food, to name a few, may also lead to this vice. In the past few years the pharmaceutical industry has put several medicines on the market, but no effective preparation that produces a lasting cure has been developed. The author is of the opinion that feather eating has a psychological basis. It most prominently manifests itself in macaws which have become sexually mature (sometime after five years of age) and have no mate. Surely, the sexual drive that arises at breeding time and finds no fulfillment is the causative factor in feather plucking. Macaws, like other large parrots, practice monogamy for the duration of their lives. Even outside the breeding season, when they are living together in small flocks with others of their species, a very close social attachment between mates can be recognized. Thus, for example, in a troop they fly very close together; and foraging, like feather care, is a joint undertaking. Nights are spent sitting close together. A macaw kept by itself must forgo all this; therefore it withdraws and becomes emotionally ill. The bad habit of feather eating rarely occurs in macaws kept in pairs or in a small troop. An animal mate is thus the best therapy for feather eating. If a second macaw cannot be kept because of lack of space or other reasons, then the single bird should be given to a breeder.

Macaws can live to an advanced age; in captivity fifty to sixty years is not rare. However, probably amazons (*Amazona*), Grey Parrots (*Psittacus erithacus*), and some cockatoos of the genera *Probosciger, Calyptorhynchus, Cacatua*, and maybe even *Callocephalon* and *Eolophus* have a longer life expectancy. Some cockatoos have been known to live more than a hundred years.

The macaw molts part of its feather coat each year. Large feathers like the flight and tail feathers are replaced within two years. The molt, which is brought about by many interdependent factors, takes place in periods of about six months. Although the macaws continually replace contour and flight feathers, the two-year molting periods, in which old, hardened feathers are shed, are evident. A similarly intense molt sets in after the breeding period. If molting should occur during the breeding period, it can cause breeding activities to break off. The replacement of feathers follows a definite pattern; that is, adjacent feathers are renewed in a temporal sequence. Simultaneous replacement of an entire group of feathers does not take place. A wing

or tail feather is shed only when the feather adjacent to it has already been replaced and has reached a certain length. Primaries, secondaries, and tail feathers can grow as much as 10 mm. per day. Molting periods mean a physical burden for a macaw, for which it compensates by increased food intake and by comparatively less activity.

On very rare occasions a bird will molt out of fright. The author first observed this violent shedding of a whole group of feathers in a Grey Parrot (*Psittacus erithacus erithacus*). The trigger for this unusual phenomenon was the shock of a mild earthquake at the edge of the Swabian Alps in 1978. Although the epicenter was almost a hundred kilometers away, the waves of tremors caused the Grey Parrot, or released a "mechanism," to drop all its tail feathers suddenly. Regrowth of feathers lost due to fright molt takes many days longer than usual, because the new feathers must first develop in the skin. In normal molting, the new, emerging feather slowly pushes the old feather out as it grows.

Since macaws are not migratory birds but stay in zones of constant climate, they do not show a special breeding plumage; the feather coat is the same throughout their lifetime, with the same number of feathers. Even young macaws already have color throughout their plumage. In macaws plumage renewal serves only to replace worn-out feathers, not, as in various other bird families, to produce breeding or winter plumage.

A numbered band attached to all birds of the order Psittaciformes (parrots) is a legal requirement [in Germany]. Importers must band the animals immediately after import, breeders a few days after hatching. Often the bands used are too tight, restricting the movement of the birds. Growths and deformities of the extremities are often the result. There is no other choice than to remove the too tight band, which is very difficult, of course. To prevent further harm to the foot, it is advisable to visit the veterinarian and have the band removed, under an anesthetic, if necessary. The removed band should, of course, be saved.

A responsible bird keeper and fancier should keep in mind the nature of the animal and offer it the best possible care and living quarters. One should always respect the creature as an individual and never "humanize" it.

1▲   2▼

1. Of the larger macaws, the Blue-and-yellow (*Ara ararauna*) has recently been the most readily available, which also fosters its popularity, no doubt. 2. One of the melanistic Blue-and-yellow Macaws bred by the Bleil family.

1. Spix's Macaw *(Cyanopsitta spixii),* on exhibit in the zoo in Naples, Italy. **2.** Hyancinth Macaws *(Anodorhynchus hyacinthinus).* **3.** Two Red-and-green Macaws *(Ara chloroptera)* engaged in preening. **4.** The shell of one kind of nut eaten in the wild by Hyacinth Macaws.

Feeding. Macaws may definitely be classified as "seed eaters." However, one should not take this too literally and offer the animals only seeds to eat. Deficiencies and illness could result from such a one-sided diet. In the wild, macaws mainly feed on the palm nuts found in their environment. They also eat other foods, such as berries, fruits, vegetables, leaf and flower buds, and grain (corn). P. Roth told the author that in September 1979, in the *pantanal* near Poconé, he saw four Hyacinth Macaws during midday "fishing" snails out of a puddle and then consuming them. However, palm fruits are of prime importance, as these nuts supply eighty percent of the daily food supply. Minerals such as sodium, calcium, magnesium, phosphorus, and calcium, and trace elements such as copper, zinc, iron, and manganese (which are absolutely needed for physiological functions) are generally found in seeds and greens only to a limited extent. Macaws in the wild bridge this gap in their mineral and trace-element requirements by ingesting mineral-rich soil. Wherever this soil is found (today mostly on sloping banks), one can often see hundreds of macaws of different species feeding together.

Food for macaws in captivity should consist of the following items: sunflower seed, various kinds of millet, canary, a little hemp, hulled rice, corn, peanuts, walnuts, hazel nuts, brazil nuts, cembra-pine nuts, wheat, oats, pumpkin seeds, and beech nuts. These foods may be regarded as basic and must always be available to the animals. The proportion of sunflower seed should amount to 40%, with the remaining kinds in varying amounts. Besides the basic foods, depending on the season, one can feed apples, pears, apricots, peaches, plums, cherries, currants, strawberries, raspberries, gooseberries, oranges, mangoes, and other fruits and vegetables, such as tomatoes, cucumbers, asparagus, spinach, lettuce, cabbage, carrots, and celery. In addition, rose hips, dandelion seed heads, various kinds of weed seeds, and rye, barley, oats, wheat, and corn are enjoyed. Branches for gnawing—from cherry, apple, pear, or willow trees—are an important extra which should not be omitted. Of course, only branches which have not been treated with insecticides should be used. Also, a piece of limestone belongs in the cage or aviary and should never be missing. Regular treats of animal protein are a very important component of a properly varied diet.

The importance of vitamins and minerals may be seen from the following list:

Vitamin A is vital for growth functions, strengthens eyesight, and affects the various skin layers. Vitamin A appears as a component of eggs, milk, and cod-liver oil, or as the precursor as carotene in carrots, corn, and kinds of cabbage.
Vitamin B$_1$ regulates carbohydrate metabolism and strengthens muscle tissue. Vitamin B$_1$ is found in yeast, egg yolk, fresh vegetables, and sprouts.
Vitamin B$_2$ regulates the conversion of nutrients and facilitates growth. Vitamin B$_2$ is a component of yeast, cod-liver oil, milk, and eggs.
Vitamin B$_6$ builds the blood and regulates growth. Vitamin B$_6$ is a component of yeast and live seed.
Vitamin B$_{12}$ is important for fat, protein, and carbohydrate metabolism and accelerates the growth of chicks. Vitamin B$_{12}$ is a component of fish and liver meals, milk, and eggs.
Vitamin C increases resistance to disease, strengthens the tissues, and activates hormones and enzymes. Vitamin C is present in fruits, vegetables, and potatoes.
Vitamin D aids bone growth and prevents thin-shelled eggs. Vitamin D is found in cod-liver oil, eggs, and milk.
Vitamin E facilitates sexual functioning (only in animals). Vitamin E is contained in live seeds or sprouts.
Vitamin H aids skin and feather formation, as well as the development of nerve cells. Vitamin H is contained in egg yolk, yeast, and molasses.
Vitamin K, the antihemorrhagic vitamin, controls blood coagulation. Vitamin K is found in vegetables, nettles, and hemp.
Iron, an important component of red blood cells, is contained in spinach, strawberries, and egg yolk.
Iodine aids thyroid functioning; it is found in cod-liver oil and garlic.
Potassium, which accelerates the growth of chicks, is contained in fruit, celery, and milk.
Calcium is important for strengthening the bones and in the nervous system; contained in edible phosphates and carbonates of lime and cuttlebone.
Copper prevents anemia and aids plumage color; found in fruit and vegetables.
Magnesium is important for strengthening bone tissue; found in spinach.
Manganese is important for growth in chicks and bone and feather growth; found in fruits and leafy vegetables.
Phosphorus, together with calcium, is the most important structural element in bone growth; contained in strawberries.

Every parrot keeper and breeder should give special attention to the composition of his birds' diet. Furnishing a food supply varied both in terms of what is offered and when is the foundation of successful animal keeping. Particularly during the acclimation period, macaws are frequently fed a one-sided diet. During this time, a multivitamin preparation should be given to the animals in their drinking water about twice each week— Completovit® (Fa. Dieckmann Arzneimittel) can be recommended. Supradyn® (Hoffmann-LaRoche) contains a substantial amount of minerals and trace elements in addition to vitamins.

Breeding. The most interesting kind of parrot keeping is a colony of several specimens of a species. Spacious flights are a prerequisite, of course; if at all possible, they should be connected to outdoor flights to which the birds have free access. By rights, parrot lovers should see themselves obliged to keep birds this way, because it is the best way to come to know the natural behavior of parrots. Almost all parrots are gregarious birds, which means that in the wild, except during the mating season, the animals congregate in troops or flocks to forage together. Macaws need companions of their own species, and in particular, they need a mate; this way, they flourish and their characteristic personality grows. Pair-bond behavior is strongly ingrained; therefore, one who keeps and fancies a single bird should come around to obtaining a mate for his "household companion."

Sometimes one is lucky in the acquisition of a second macaw; one of the opposite sex is obtained, and a pair can be put together. An even better approach, provided that one is financially able and has sufficient accommodations at his disposal, would be to put together at the same time four to six macaws of the same species (and if at all possible, of the same race). This kind of set-up offers optimal conditions for successful and productive breeding.

In the wild, macaws live in flocks and thus are subject to the rules of social behavior. Their attempts under captive conditions to mate with bird species from other orders shows that some behavior patterns are not innate but are acquired during the so-called sensitive period of imprinting. This

sensitive period (i.e., the time when parent birds or conspecifics transmit behavior patterns to youngsters) is, with macaws probably, the time between birth and the onset of sexual maturity. If macaws are kept in an unnatural situation during this learning period (being kept in captivity is unnatural, being kept as a single bird especially so), then it may be expected that misimprinting will occur through social isolation. After the onset of sexual maturity, it is difficult for misimprinted macaws to integrate into a flock or to find mates. However, the author knows of some successful attempts in which misimprinted large parrots were brought together with other members of their species. The breeding pairs that emerged produced offspring in the second season or later and thereafter did so regularly. In the larger parrot species, the learning process is not rigidly fixed after the sensitive period, consequently there is always the possibility, as well as the need, to attempt to breed singly-kept macaws.

A positive method for putting together pairs is endoscopic sex determination. There are veterinarians who specialize in such work (see the section on sex determination). Of course, macaws are very discriminating in their choice of mates, and it may happen that only the second or third possible mate is accepted; only then will a compatible pair result.

Another obstacle in the way of offspring is that many macaw species are not capable of breeding until they are five or six years old. In the smaller macaw species, sexual maturity generally occurs after four years of age, but occasionally as early as after two years. If one obtains young birds for breeding, he will have to have a great deal of patience until the birds are finally ready for breeding. Important prerequisites for successful breeding are a compatible macaw pair (which are hand-tame, if possible) at least six years old, and accustomed to an extremely varied diet.

A crucial factor contributing to successful breeding is the kind of shelter. The best opportunity is afforded by a large outdoor flight with a shelter room, in a quiet place, with suitable and varied perches. For the interior, one should forswear the sterility commonly practiced and make the furnishings as varied and copious as possible. A diversified environment for the macaws can be

1, 4. Illiger's Macaw (*Ara maracana*). Franz Veser owns what is probably the most productive macaw breeding pair of all. The lower photo shows the breeding pair preening, with four youngsters sitting nearby. 2. Military Macaw (*Ara militaris*). This bird came from Mexico, so, despite the throat coloration, it must belong to the subspecies *mexicana*. 3. The behavior apparent in this photo—the one bird sitting low, while the other perches upright with body feathers raised—may indicate that these Chestnut-fronted Macaws (*Ara severa*) are a pair, the upright one being the male.

28

Cages made of wrought iron are currently popular for accommodating macaws in the home. In this instance, the occupant is a Military Macaw *(Ara militaris)*.

provided with old, rotted tree trunks placed about, little walls of natural stones, hidden perching places, and forest soil scattered around—the floor of the flight can be covered with soil and a layer of sand can be poured under the perches. If the flight was constructed with double wire mesh, then the outer mesh can be planted with vegetation that will climb swiftly and grow around the flight; this affords further concealment and gives the animals further opportunity to flourish undisturbed. Food dishes should be installed so that they can be reached from the outside without difficulty. By means of a small water pump, one can install a fountain or small waterfall which will simultaneously provide water for drinking and the necessary high humidity.

Attractive nest boxes can be made out of tree trunks, set up in a dry part of the aviary, if possible, and protected from wind and rain. The larger macaws should have nest boxes with an interior diameter of about 50 cm. and a height of about 120 cm. The entrance hole should be in the upper third of the nest box and should have a diameter of 20–25 cm. In addition, a door about 20 x 20 cm in the log will make nest inspection possible. For the smaller macaws, nest boxes with an interior diameter of about 30–35 cm. and a height of 60–70 cm. are satisfactory. Of course, nest boxes made out of wooden boards will serve the same purpose. It is very important to put some kind of ladder inside the nest box so that the birds can climb down to the floor. Place a layer 6–10 cm. thick of decayed wood chips and wood shavings in the box. When the macaws seem ready to breed, offer them two or three nest boxes to choose from; as soon as they have decided on one, the others can be removed.

The courtship display of macaws is not especially rich in variety, but it does present an interesting spectacle to the observer. For example, the pupils of the eye contract to pin-point size, and during courting the animals' bare cheek patches, particularly in males of the genus *Ara*, will turn red. In all species of the four genera, the intimidation behavior of the cocks is ingrained. At the approach of their keeper or of visitors, they flap their wings and jump back and forth on the perch in front of the hen. Intimidation by the cocks often increases, and mock attacks on the keeper are not unusual.

The courtship of macaws can last from two to four weeks; by the end of this period, copulation will be taking place daily and, for the most part, at the same time each day. Successful copulations are rare; therefore, as a rule, macaws must copulate frequently during the courtship and egg-laying period. Spermatoza are viable for up to ten days. Since macaw hens have about a three-day interval in egg laying, it may happen that not all of the eggs will be fertile, either because copulation was not successful or because the sperm had lost their ability to fertilize, even before the yolk was enclosed in its albumen layer.

The macaw hen lays her eggs at three-day intervals. In the case of the smaller macaw species, the egg-laying interval may vary from two to three days, with a clutch consisting of as many as five eggs. With the larger macaw species, it is rare that more than three eggs are laid; as a rule, there are only two eggs. Macaw eggs are small and light in relation to the body weight of the birds, having a weight of about 3.5–4.0% of the weight of the hen. By comparison, a Budgerigar (*Melopsittacus undulatus*) hen produces eggs that can amount to as much as 8% of the bird's weight. The eggshell of almost all birds of the order Psittaciformes is pure white. During the incubation period, the broad oval eggs take on a light color, which comes from the nesting material present.

The female begins incubating immediately after the first egg is laid. During the incubation period, the male often climbs into the nest box and will remain there temporarily, but does not take part in the actual incubation. The hen leaves the nest for short periods only in order to feed and to relieve herself. Sometimes one can observe that the female is fed by the male. The incubation period lasts for approximately twenty-six days. If the clutch has been incubated tightly, from the first egg, a naked, blind chick will emerge at the end of this time. After a few minutes of life, the chicks make soft peeping sounds. During the first few days, the nestlings are for the most part fed only by the female. During this time, the cock will usually feed the hen plentifully, but seldom, if ever, the chicks. When the chicks have reached the age of about three weeks, the male will take a direct part in feeding the young. During the first few days of life, the chicks should be inspected in the nest box to determine whether they are being fed and taken care of. The parents will react to nest inspection with extreme aggression and belligerence toward the keeper.

During the rearing of the young, a complete, nourishing diet must be supplied, because a one-sided diet can produce young birds with signs of deficiency. Some macaws will frequently eat a very one-sided diet for a long period of time, restricting themselves to sunflower seeds or nuts. Once the incubation and brooding period has begun, this behavior changes, and suddenly the birds will eat virtually all foods offered.

The chicks open their eyes at about two weeks of age, and at the same time rapid feather growth begins. Soon the first colored plumage areas can be recognized. The beak of the chick, which is often a light color, gradually changes, reaching its final coloration shortly before fledging. Nestling periods vary widely. In the case of the smaller species, rearing lasts about ten weeks. With larger species, the nestling period can last as long as a hundred days. The youngsters are independent a few days after fledging, although their parents still continue to feed them for a time.

It is important that the fledglings be allowed to remain with their parents. Only when conflict arises between parents and offspring should the young be separated. Still, one should not make the mistake of removing the youngsters so that they are completely out of sight of their parents. This would significantly hamper the behavioral development of the young, putting them on the wrong track completely. In the wild, youngsters are guided by adult birds (especially their parents) for many months after leaving the nest and becoming independent; in this way, they are socially imprinted. It is, therefore, absolutely necessary to house progeny in an flight adjacent to their parents, to guarantee that species-characteristic behavior patterns will be acquired by the subadult birds through visual contact.

To hand-rear macaws is an extremely difficult undertaking. Every bird fancier who strives to breed his animals is sooner or later confronted with the problem that newly hatched chicks are sometimes not satisfactorily cared for by the parents or are even abandoned. As a responsible keeper, one is obligated to undertake the rearing of such young

himself. The prognosis that a chick a few days old will be reared successfully is naturally quite unfavorable; in many cases the outcome is negative.

The main problems in hand-rearing are providing rearing food of the right composition, appropriate feeding techniques, and meeting the chick's needs for warmth. The ideal rearing temperature is about 33 C. Care must be taken to avoid having hot spots, and the warm air should be circulated constantly. The appropriate temperature can be achieved with a small electric heater or an incubator. The incubator has the advantage over the electric heater in that a constant, steady temperature can be maintained and that the humidity—which should be at about 80%—can be regulated. Experiments at the Wuppertaler Zoo showed that even when temperature and humidity were kept almost constant, macaw chicks had indigestion.

The composition of the feeding mixture is of greatest importance and makes an essential contribution to the success of hand-rearing. The food mixture chosen by the Wuppertaler Zoo for hand-rearing macaw hybrids may be considered an optimum rearing food. By slightly modifying the composition of this mixture and the way it is prepared, the author was able to hand-raise amazons successfully. The hand-rearing food consists of the following ingredients: a half cup of shredded wheat mixed with two egg yolks and two tablespoons of powdered milk, then thinned out with a little water to make a soupy mixture. The mixture is heated over a small flame until it develops a firm consistency. After it cools, curd cheese and bananas are added in the following proportions: 3/4 of the above mixture, 1/8 bananas, and 1/8 curd cheese. This mixture is somewhat soft, so some soft, half-ripe corn (when available), sprouted seeds, and a few oil seeds may be included. Either T-Vitamin-Götch®, Polyvital®, Sanostol®, Multimulsin®, or some other vitamin preparation can be added. The calcium requirement can be satisfied with a small amounts of grated cuttlebone, edible calcium, or Calcipot®. The food mixture must be warmed to body temperature. Naturally, other kinds of foods and mixtures can be used as well. Baby food—made by Alete, Hipp and other companies, for example—can be the fundamental ingredient of a rearing food, to which one adds ground and sprouted seeds, fruit, vegetables, honey, oatmeal, etc.

1, 2. Illiger's Macaw *(Ara maracana)*. In the nest box with the hen, these chicks bred by F. Veser range in age from 10 to 16 days. Their age as they are being weighed is 20 to 25 days. **3.** Yellow-collared Macaw *(Ara auricollis)* being reared artificially, using an eyedropper.

Feeding small chicks is not easy and is often risky. For the youngsters' first few days, a so-called one-way syringe can be used for feeding. The nozzle of the syringe can be widened and a bicycle-tire valve stem about 3 cm. long attached. The syringe barrel is filled with the prepared food; then feeding can begin. The valve stem is put a short way into the beak of the macaw chick, then the plunger of the syringe is very cautiously depressed, so that the mixture slowly flows into the animal's crop. With this method of feeding there is always a relatively great danger that the food will be squirted into the windpipe. A food mixture squirted into the windpipe can cause immediate death. For this reason alone, it is recommended that, as soon as possible, you switch from this feeding method to using a reshaped teaspoon. Bend the sides of the spoon up high, so that a shovel-shaped utensil is produced. For the most part, chicks can be fed by spoon without difficulty after they are fifteen days old.

During the first three weeks, feedings should take place at intervals of about two hours. If possible, this routine should be continued even at night. After about ten days of age, feeding intervals may be lengthened to about three hours, and it is then possible to give the last feeding between eleven p.m. and midnight and the first morning feeding at about 6 a.m. The older the chick becomes, the greater the time intervals possible between feedings. Thus, by the time the chicks are about to fledge, food need be provided only four times daily. After every feeding, clean the macaw chick so that any food particles clinging to the body are removed. At the same time, one should clean the artificial nest. The nest set-up is very important. When you provide a bare nest floor, there is a danger that the toes of the chick will be deformed. Therefore, the floor of the artificial nest should be covered with wood chips, shavings, straw, or hay. The macaw chick can then grasp this material with its toes, so that no defects or deformities will occur.

Hand-raising a parrot is quite a task for the keeper, but in the long run it affords him knowledge and experience which no bird fancier should be without.

Sex Determination. Setting up suitable macaw pairs is quite difficult because with nearly all species of the genera *Anordorhychus, Cyanopsitta, Ara,* and *Diopsittaca,* no external differences between males and females can be discerned. An exception, though with limitations, is Illiger's Macaw (*Ara maracana*), in which cocks generally exhibit more red in the plumage of the forehead, the belly, and the back. Still, one must compare several birds to pick out a pair. One may also draw conclusions about the sex of a bird from long observation of its behavior. Males more frequently exhibit more aggressive behavior; as a rule, their carriage is more upright; and they are more positive toward change. Even courtship behavior in sexually mature animals is an unreliable sign, since homosexuality can occur between animals of the same sex, so that two males or two females copulate with one another. Similarly uncertain are a higher crown, a broader bill, and greater body length as characteristics of a cock. A well-built hen will sooner be taken for a cock than will a more frail male bird. In regard to determining sex by feeling the pelvic bones, females shortly before and after egg laying (and only at this time!) show a greater space between the junction of the pubic bones and the tip of the breastbone; but this in effect means little, since it is clear anyhow that a hen is involved when an egg is laid.

All of the possible ways of sex determination mentioned presuppose that at the time several animals of a species or race will be kept together, so that conclusions about their sex can be drawn from their behavior patterns or characteristics. Certainly the acquisition of a group of birds of the same species is the best prerequisite for successful, productive breeding later. Macaws very likely practice monogamy for life; for this reason they are very discriminating in their choice of a mate. The theory that any male and female are a pair and that nothing else will stand in the way of offspring does not apply to macaws. The author has often seen that guaranteed males and females did not get along and productive pair bonding was out of the question.

Only a few fanciers are in a position to put together a whole group of macaws so that they can acquire a pair for breeding purposes. With a new technique, so-called endoscopy, examination of the testes and ovaries provides a hundred-percent successful method of sex determination. Many veterinarians are currently able to sex birds with this procedure. Using a drug in a dosage adjusted to the body weight of the "patient," the bird to be examined is anesthetized until it reaches a totally relaxed state. The bird is then placed on its right side, and the left wing is lifted up, while the left leg is stretched toward the rear. With a scalpel, an incision about 3 mm. long is made in the middle of the space below the ribs (the feathers in this area will have been removed previously). The endoscope can now be inserted as far as the gonads (between the lung tissue and the kidneys). Ovaries or testicles are easily recognized, for the most part. After sex has been determined, the endoscope is carefully removed and the small incision sewn shut. The bird should then be brought back to its familiar environment as quickly as possible. For the following week the endoscopically examined bird should be observed constantly, so that any possible complications that may occur can be treated immediately. Endoscopy is the most certain method of sex determination; it may be employed with rare birds that are not externally sexually dimorphic. It should be mentioned once more that a definite pair is still not necessarily a pair that will breed.

Breeders and dealers employ a conventional notation to indicate sex. For example, if one pair is for sale, the indication is 1,1. Males are indicated before the comma, females after. 1,0 means that only one cock is in question, while 0,1 means one hen. Five males and six females would be offered with the designation 5,6. A second form of notation may be found in articles and books: ♀ =female, and ♂ =male.

Breeding Licenses. In 1975 [in Germany], a law for protection against psittacosis and ornithosis, the so-called Psittacosis Law, was promulgated (and published in the *Bundesgesetzblatt* Jahrgang 1975, Teil 1). Breeders of parrots (parrots being all birds placed in the order Psittaciformes of the zoological classification) are required by law to obtain a license for breeding before they can maintain a breeding facility. Local authorities are charged with the issuance of licenses. To obtain such a license, certain requirements must be met. The applicant must have the necessary specialized knowledge for the care and maintainance of parrots and have been thoroughly instructed in the animal-protection laws and the Psittacosis Law. A suitable amount of space

must be available for breeding and communal housing, and the area must be arranged so that in the event of an outbreak of a contagious disease, it may be effectively controlled, with the help of the authorities. The license will be granted only after these mandatory requirements are fulfilled; it is granted in writing and can be withdrawn if conditions change.

Breeders are further obligated to maintain an official breeding register, entering the acquisition, sale, and banding of offspring, as well as the treatment of any diseases which may afflict the animals. For banding the offspring, the required leg bands may be obtained, for example, at the Zentralverband Zoologischer Fachgeschäfte Deutschlands e. V. in Frankfurt, after the receipt of the official breeding license. As required by the epizootic law (§61d, Abs. 1), the following information must be entered in the register book:

(1) Species of animal.
(2) Band number and date of banding.
(3) Date of acquisition or other receipt (breeding), as well as the provenance of the animals.
(4) Date of surrender and recipient of the animal, or date of death of the animal.
(5) Initiation, duration, and results of treatment against psitticosis, as well as kind of medicine and dosage used.

The register books can also be obtained through the Zentralverband (ZZA) or from a registered breeders' association, such as the AZ, after a breeding license has been issued. New register books must be immediately taken to the responsible authority to be officially stamped and recorded. Every breeder is obligated to preserve the breeding book for at least two years after the last entry.

It is worth knowing that the official veterinarian has the authority to enter the premises in which parrots (birds of the order Psittaciformes) are kept, in order, if necessary, to examine the animals and to assess their accommodations. If special measures are needed for the diagnosis of disease, then this will be done under the direction of the official veterinarian.

The author would like to point out that not every aviary facility can successfully combat a disease. Therefore, it is recommended that in building a large breeding facility one should construct a so-called quarantine station at the same time, an area off to the side—made of tiles, if possible—with its own water and drainage system. In the event of a disease outbreak, all animals can be housed and treated together in the quarantine station. Furthermore, this area offers the possibility of maintaining new birds separately for observation and, in the event of disease, treating them separately from other birds. In this way, the incidence of a disease which could threaten the entire stock of birds can be averted almost completely.

Illness. Though macaws are robust, hearty birds, in cage and aviary they are nonetheless constantly exposed to dangers which can lead to disease or injury. As the keeper of these interesting birds of the genera *Anodorhynchus, Cyanopsitta, Ara,* and *Diopsittaca,* one should feel obligated to follow basic hygienic practices in their care and accommodations. If injury or disease does occur, one should seek out the cause and immediately begin treatment of the sick or injured animal. In general, if there is an outbreak of disease, a veterinarian should be consulted. Many diseases manifest the same external symptoms, so that a superficial examination can result in an inaccurate diagnosis. A quick cure can be expected only if sick or injured birds are promptly treated by a veterinarian while they are to some extent still in good physical condition.

The sick macaws should be separated from any other birds present and, if necessary, housed in a hospital cage. If one member of a compatible macaw pair becomes ill, then the healthy bird should be placed in the hospital cage together with the sick one, since separation would be an extra burden on the sick bird.

In birds, as a rule, illness becomes evident quickly. Obvious signs of illness include perching quietly, dull eyes, constant sleeping, decreased activity, droppings stuck to the vent, drainage from the nostrils and blocked nostrils, heavy breathing, shortness of breath, lameness, abnormal movements, diarrhea, constipation, swollen eyelids, emaciation, etc.—these signs can easily be noticed by anyone who regularly observes his birds.

Medicines prescribed by the veterinarian are to be given in the appropriate dosage at the recommended time. The amount of medicine to be used depends in part on the body weight of the bird. If at all possible, with mild illnesses use natural medicines derived from herbs. Severe illnesses, however, can

be treated successfully only by using powerful, quick-acting medicines. Unfortunately, every disease and its background cannot be covered in this book, but relevant specialized literature is listed in the bibliography.

Some diseases will be considered here, since they can be life-threatening to the birds and under certain conditions can also present a danger to people. The following accounts of diseases are taken from my book on amazon parrots.

Psittacosis/Ornithosis. Parrot fever (psittacosis) is a viral infection which can take on epizootic forms and which can also cause illness in humans. In 1874, it was noted that contact with diseased parrots transmitted the disease to people. Many individuals who contracted the disease died. In 1934, the so-called Psittacosis Law was put into effect and at the same time caused all infected parrot stocks to be depopulated. Following the development by the pharmaceutical industry of effective medicines and in view of the successful rate of cures that could be achieved, a law was promulgated by the cabinet minister for Food, Agriculture, and Forests on October 1, 1970: the Ordinance for Protection against Psittacosis and Ornithosis (Psittacosis Ordinance). In spite of the intensive tetracycline treatment of parrots newly imported into Germany, 200 to 300 cases of human infection are reported annually. Every outbreak, or even the suspicion of the presence psittacosis, must be reported to the proper authority, as well as to the official veterinarian. As a breeder and keeper of parrots, it is one's obligation to have his stock of birds examined for psittacosis at least once a year, as a preventive measure. All state laboratories conduct such tests from freshly collected stool specimens. Because psittacosis is contagious and widespread, it is recommended that newly acquired parrots always be segregated and acclimated in separate accommodations. At the same time, freshly collected stool specimens should be delivered to the laboratory for testing. Newly acquired birds should be put together with other birds only when it is a hundred percent certain that the new arrival is healthy. Always keep in mind that the introduction of psittacosis organisms can cause the entire stock of healthy birds to become sick or to die, within a very short time. In addition, always keep in mind that the virus presents a serious and perhaps even deadly threat to people.

The clinical picture of psittacosis in the parrot shows very unspecific signs, which in the early stages can often lead to a false diagnosis. Often one can recognize the illness by a viscous nasal discharge, lack of appetite, and labored and heavy breathing. Furthermore, the diseased birds appear apathetic, sleep constantly, and are fluffed up when they perch. Such signs, however, also appear with other diseases. Therefore, in order to be assured of an unequivocal diagnosis, one should immediately collect fresh stool specimens from the sick animal and send them to a state laboratory. Should the results of the tests confirm the suspicion of psittacosis, treatment must commence immediately. In addition, the directives of the official veterinarian must be followed.

Good cures can be achieved with a soft food containing chlortetracycline, providing a fresh mixture daily. With the smaller parrots and parakeets, the preparation is given for thirty days; larger parakeets and parrots receive it for forty-five days. Macaws that have acute psittacosis and refuse nourishment must first be treated by injection. A one-time injection of 300 mg. of an oil-based solution of Chloromycetin® (chloramphenicol) or similar antibiotic will be sufficient in most cases. Following this, most birds will eat again. To obtain a cure, one continues the medicated food. Effective treatment will produce a blood level of 1.0 mcg/ml. from a blood sample taken on the tenth day of treatment.

Salmonellosis (Paratyphoid). *Salmonella* infections can occur in animals and people. These microorganisms are always communicable, even to birds. The bacteria, of which 1600 different species are known, can be shed by so-called carriers, people or animals who outwardly appear completely healthy, at irregular time intervals. These disease carriers constitute the greatest source of danger for a healthy bird. In addition, the danger of salmonellosis always exists, even when macaws are kept singly. Infected people, utensils, cages, etc., constantly present a risk. The clinical picture of salmonellosis is quite varied; only through laboratory testing can the disease be unequivocally diagnosed. In the acute intestinal form of

salmonellosis, the diseased animals will perch listlessly and suffer from diarrhea with extremely loose droppings. The cerebral form produces disturbances of the nervous system, and victims are frequently afflicted with lameness and cramps. The so-called arthritic form, a chronic form of the disease, is recognizable by wing or leg crippling. In the case of live animals, as was mentioned, certain diagnosis is possible only through laboratory examination of the droppings, from which the bacteria may be isolated.

Following diagnosis, antibiotic treatment which will lead to the recovery of the ill birds should be initiated. The initial dose of the medicine should be injected, as this is the quickest way to achieve a proper level of the medicine in the tissues. Further treatment should be undertaken via the food or drinking water. Animals suffering from salmonellosis should generally be housed in a separate location. All objects in the vicinity of the cage should be disinfected every other day until the conclusion of the treatment. Fourteen days after the end of treatment, a test of the droppings must again be done in the laboratory in order to confirm the success of the treatment.

Newcastle Disease (Fowl Pest). In recent years there have been repeated outbreaks of fowl pest. Newcastle disease was observed not only in poultry, but also in other birds, including parrots. This viral infection can run a devastating course and do a tremendous amount of damage to a stock of birds in a very short time. Four or five days after infection, the animals manifest a loss of appetite and a rise in body temperature. The animals hide in darkened corners and exhibit watery diarrhea, labored breathing, and ruffled feathers. Neurological reactions may also be observed: rotating the head 180 degrees, lameness, and cramps (Dr. Aeckerlein). The signs and the course of the disease can vary greatly, so it is difficult to recognize it. Transmission to other birds can occur through air, utensils, or dust. Certain diagnosis is possible only from a dead animal, through evidence of the virus or a hemagglutination-inhibition test. As with all viral infections, no treatment seems to be possible. It is known, however, that the disease organism shows less resistance when exposed to strong ultraviolet radiation. Therefore, it is recommended as a preventive and as supportive treatment that the birds be housed in bright daylight and, possibly, that supplementary ultraviolet lighting be provided. Extra doses of vitamins can also strengthen the bird's own defenses. A law requiring the inoculation of new imports with a vaccine while they are in the quarantine station has been under consideration, because only through such a systematic preventive campaign can further incidence and spread of the disease be limited effectively.

Worms. In larger breeding facilities there is always the danger of diseases involving worms. It is well known that birds in the wild are often subject to various worm parasites. An attack of worms in aviary birds can have the most severe consequences and, under certain circumstances, can result in the loss of the entire stock of birds. The incidence and spread of parasitic worms is always possible. A parasitefree stock can become completely infested by worms by the introduction of one bird carrying worms. For example, a female roundworm produces several thousand eggs per day, which the bird then excretes. With favorable temperatures and sufficient moisture, conditions which are always present in an aviary, the eggs develop into viable larvae. Birds foraging and feeding on the aviary floor may ingest the worm larvae. To keep one's birds permanently free of worms, one must observe at least the minimal hygienic requirements when constructing

the aviary and in keeping the premises and its accessories clean. Roundworms (ascarids) and threadworms (*Capillaria* spp.) are widespread and can often cause the death of an afflicted bird.

In most cases, there is no special clinical picture for a bird with a worm infestation; without regular examination of the birds' droppings, diagnosis is impossible. Depending on the kind of parasite, specific medicines are available to treat worm infestations (e.g., Dekelmin® or Eustidil®). The correct dosage can be obtained by consulting the instructions accompanying the medicine. A follow-up of the same preparation may be given four weeks after the initial treatment. With a small stock of birds, the medicine should be given directly: by means of an eyedropper or injected into the breast muscles.

Parallel with the medication, the aviary itself and all utensils must be disinfected. Earth floors must be turned over to a depth of about 20 cm. Trellises, food and water dishes, perches, and other aviary equipment should be treated with a disinfecting agent (Dekaseptol®, for example). Possibly the nonflammable parts of the aviary can be heated briefly with a propane torch. As already mentioned, with constantly changing stock, or with parrots kept in outdoor flights, droppings should be examined regularly. Newly acquired birds should generally be kept in acclimation cages. Only after one is sure that the animals are healthy and wormfree can they be transferred to aviaries with other birds.

The Genera and Species

The Systematic Position of the Macaws.
Systematically, the order of parrots (Psittaciformes)
is a separate, completely distinct group in the large
class of birds (Aves), having very few kindred
relationships to other orders of birds. Systematists
list the parrots after the pigeons (order
Columbiformes); following the parrots are the owls
(order Strigiformes). Recently, Hans Edmund
Wolters has taken James Lee Peters's 1937 *Check-
list of Birds of the World*, which has not been
completed, and revised the listing according to the
most recent views. The author does not agree with
every placement in the new list, nor does he
recognize the phyletic arrangement of the new
system of classification, which in one instance links
Pesquet's Parrot (*Psittrichas*), the Kakapo (*Strigops*),
perhaps the Palm Cockatoo (*Probosciger*) and
certainly the Nestoridae; yet he believes that the
taxonomic arrangement of the new classification is a
signpost for the future. Thus the sequence of this
new check-list is the basis for the treatment of the
macaws in this book.

The order of parrots is divided into eleven
families, which are in part composed of subfamilies.
The macaw genera are placed in the family
Psittacidae, which consists of eight subfamilies;
these in turn are composed of the various genera.
The macaw genera are the first four of eighteen
genera in the second subfamily, the Aratinginae.
The various genera are composed of species; also,
some species may be made up of different
geographic races.

Macaws are placed in the following genera:
Anodorhynchus, Cyanopsitta, Ara, and *Diopsittaca.*
In the species list below, the enumeration is
designed to include species already extinct; however,
they are placed at the beginning of the sequence.

ANODORHYNCHUS
- 0. *Anodorhynchus purpurascens,*
  Violet Macaw (doubtful species)
- 1. *Anodorhynchus hyacinthinus,*
  Hyacinth Macaw
- 2. *Anodorhynchus glaucus,*
  Glaucous Macaw
- 3. *Anodorhynchus leari,*
  Lear's Macaw

CYANOPSITTA
- 1. *Cyanopsitta spixii,*
  Spix's Macaw

ARA
- 0. *Ara tricolor,*
  Cuban Macaw (extinct)
- 0. *Ara atwoodi,*
  Dominican Macaw (extinct)
- 0. *Ara autocthones,*
  St. Croix Macaw (extinct)
- 0. *Ara erythrura,*
  Mysterious Macaw (extinct)
- 0. *Ara erythrocephala,*
  Green-and-yellow Macaw (extinct)
- 0. *Ara gossei,*
  Yellow-headed Macaw (extinct)
- 0. *Ara guadeloupensis,*
  Guadeloupe Red Macaw (extinct)
- 0. *Ara martinica,*
  Orange-bellied Macaw (extinct)

1st Group: *Sittace*
- 1. *Ara glaucogularis,*
  Blue-throated Macaw
- 2. *Ara ararauna,*
  Blue-and-yellow Macaw

2nd Group
- 3. *Ara rubrogenys,*
  Red-fronted Macaw

3rd Group: *Hemipsittacus*
- 4. *Ara severa,*
  Chestnut-fronted Macaw (two subspecies)

4th Group: *Primolius*
    5. *Ara auricollis,*
       Yellow-collared Macaw
    6. *Ara couloni,*
       Blue-headed Macaw
    7. *Ara maracana,*
       Illiger's Macaw
5th Group: *Orthopsittaca*
    8. *Ara manilata,*
       Red-bellied Macaw
6th Group: *Ara*
    9. *Ara militaris,*
       Military Macaw (three subspecies)
   10. *Ara ambigua,*
       Great Green Macaw (two subspecies)
7th Group: *Ara*
   11. *Ara chloroptera,*
       Red-and-green Macaw
   12. *Ara macao,*
       Scarlet Macaw

DIOPSITTACA
    1. *Diopsittaca nobilis,*
       Red-shouldered Macaw (three subspecies)

   3. *Ara militaris,*
       Military Macaw (three subspecies)
   4. *Ara ambigua,*
       Great Green Macaw (two subspecies)
   5. *Ara macao,*
       Scarlet Macaw
   6. *Ara chloroptera,*
       Red-and-green Macaw
   7. *Ara tricolor,*
       Cuban Macaw (extinct)
   8. *Ara rubro-genys,*
       Red-fronted Macaw
   9. *Ara auricollis,*
       Yellow-collared Macaw
  10. *Ara severa,*
       Chestnut-fronted Macaw (two subspecies)
  11. *Ara (Cyanopsitta) spixii,*
       Spix's Macaw
  12. *Ara manilata,*
       Red-bellied Macaw
  13. *Ara maracana,*
       Illiger's Macaw
  14. *Ara couloni,*
       Blue-headed Macaw
  15. *Ara nobilis,*
       Red-shouldered Macaw (three subspecies)

The species list prepared by James Lee Peters should be mentioned, for in a slightly altered form his *Check-list of Birds of the World* will be useful in the future on an international level. According to Peters, the order of parrots (Psittaciformes) contains a single family, the Psittacidae. This family is composed of five subfamilies, some of which consist of generic groups. The macaws are placed in the fourth subfamily, the Psittacinae. For Peters, the macaws constitute two genera:

ANODORHYNCHUS
    1. *Anodorhynchus hyacinthinus,*
       Hyacinth Macaw
    2. *Anodorhynchus glaucus,*
       Glaucous Macaw
    3. *Anodorhynchus leari,*
       Lear's Macaw

ARA
    1. *Ara ararauna,*
       Blue-and-yellow Macaw
    2. *Ara caninde (glaucogularis),*
       Blue-throated Macaw

This listing shows that Peters's arrangement is in need of revision. Wolters's check-list could be an essential first step toward a new classification in the future. The distinctness of the various geographic races in the different species is problematical, however. Scientists often describe a new subspecies on the basis of the most minute, barely detectable differences, such as smaller size or hardly noticeable differences in plumage coloration (as in *Ara severa,* for example). Also, the separation of three species of blue macaws (*Anodorhynchus*) seems doubtful to the author. More probably, there is a single species composed of three geographic races: a northern (*Anodorhynchus hyacinthinus leari*), a central (*A. hyacinthinus hyacinthinus*), and a southern (*A. hyacinthinus glaucus*). This thesis is supported by the distinctly separate ranges as well as the extreme size differences among these macaws. Further scientific research employing available skins, as well as behavioral studies of live birds (courtship and breeding habits, vocalizations, and other behavior patterns), could contribute an essential clarification to these controversial questions.

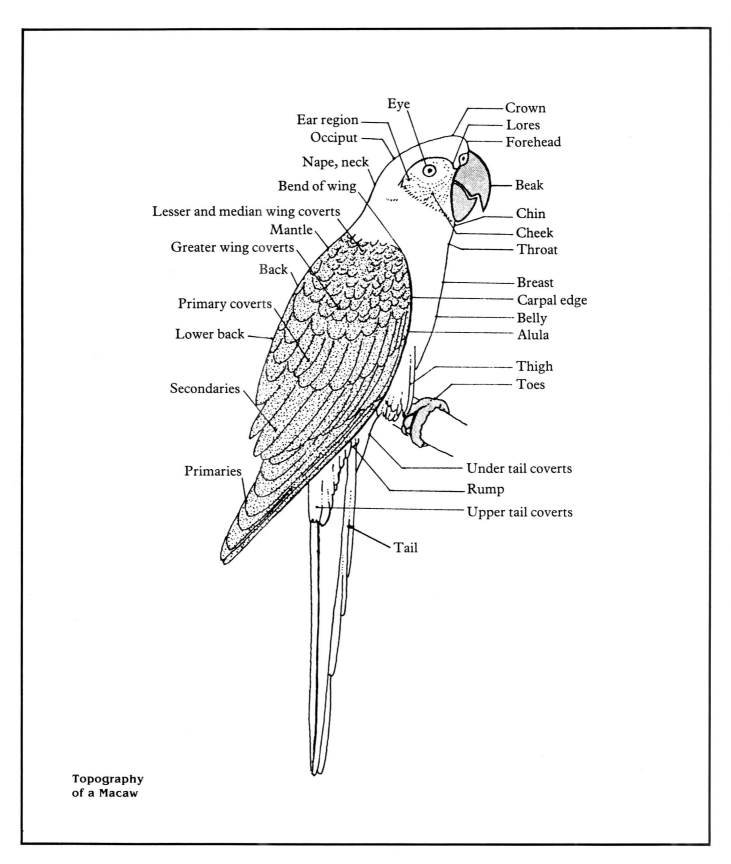

Eye
Crown
Ear region
Lores
Occiput
Forehead
Nape, neck
Beak
Bend of wing
Chin
Lesser and median wing coverts
Cheek
Mantle
Throat
Greater wing coverts
Breast
Back
Carpal edge
Primary coverts
Belly
Lower back
Alula
Thigh
Secondaries
Toes
Primaries
Under tail coverts
Rump
Upper tail coverts
Tail

**Topography
of a Macaw**

Macaws, especially those of the genera *Ara* and *Diopsittaca*, are closely related to some other genera of the subfamily Aratinginae. The chief, most apparent characteristics distinguishing these species from those of other genera are the naked facial patch and the size of the long tail. The genus *Aratinga* is probably the most closely related to the macaws, though the wing is longer than the tail in *Aratinga* species. The Blue-crowned Conure (*Thectocercus acuticaudatus*, formerly *Aratinga acuticaudata*) is an exception: its tail length exceeds wing length by about ten percent. The genus *Anodorhynchus* with its three blue species also holds a somewhat isolated position; however, it is possible to regard the genus *Cyanopsitta* as intermediate between *Ara* and *Anodorhynchus*. A point worth noting is that, compared to other parrot species, the *Ara* species have few geographic races. If one examines the richly varied coloration of *Ara macao*, *Ara chloroptera*, and *Ara ararauna*, he may be tempted to assume that some regional forms can be regarded as subspecies. The widespread distribution, particularly in the case of the three species mentioned, further supports this thesis.

Unfortunately, those scientists working in the field of ornithology tend to treat parrots as stepchildren and pay very little attention this interesting order of birds. Though amateur ornithologists and breeders the world over constantly publish articles about parrots in specialist magazines and contribute their extensive knowledge about the behavior of these birds in captivity, thus far, their observations have been used little by professional ornithologists.

Genus *ANODORHYNCHUS* Spix, 1824

Three very large species of parrots are grouped in the genus *Anodorhynchus* on the basis of their characteristics. The most pronounced difference from the genus *Ara* is their striking bare eye ring, as well as the naked area at the base of the lower mandible, usually colored either yellow or orange yellow. The cere, lores, and cheeks are completely feathered. The arrangement of the bones of the skull, especially around the ear, differs in structure from related forms. The plumage color of all three species is uniformly blue, in different shades. There do not appear to be any clearly evident differences between males and females. Similarly, young birds cannot be distinguished from adults.

Violet Macaw *Anodorhynchus purpurascens* Rothschild 1905

Range. Guadaloupe (West Indies)

Remarks. Rothschild's (1905) description relies on a report by Don de Navaret (1838) which very possibly gives either superficial information about the already extinct Violet Amazon (*Amazona violaceus*) or refers to one of the South American blue macaws (*Anodorhynchus*). The original description of the bird indicated that it was colored a deep violet. Its name is *oné couli*. Rothschild places the parrot in the genus *Anodorhynchus* on the basis of the plumage description.

Hyacinth Macaw *Anodorhynchus hyacinthinus* Latham 1790

Characteristics. Size, about 100 cm. Cobalt blue. Head, sides of neck, and front side somewhat lighter cobalt blue. Underside of primaries and secondaries as well as the underside of the tail feathers blackish blue. Bare band of skin on the base of the lower mandible and bare eye ring orange yellow. Iris black. Beak black. Toes brown black. Female like the male, perhaps somewhat more slender. Young birds like adults, but somewhat more slender.

Range. Brazil: southeastern Pará, central and eastern Mato Grosso, central and northern Goiás, northwestern Minas Gerais, western Bahia, southwestern Piauí, and southernmost Maranhão.

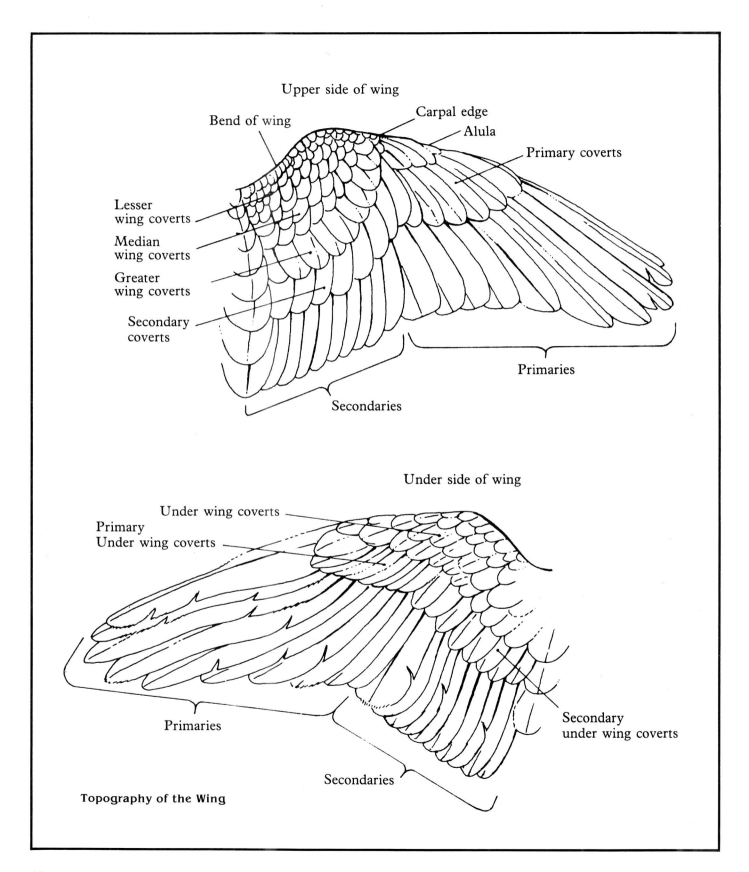

Topography of the Wing

Upper side of wing

Bend of wing

Carpal edge

Alula

Primary coverts

Lesser wing coverts

Median wing coverts

Greater wing coverts

Secondary coverts

Secondaries

Primaries

Under side of wing

Under wing coverts

Primary Under wing coverts

Primaries

Secondaries

Secondary under wing coverts

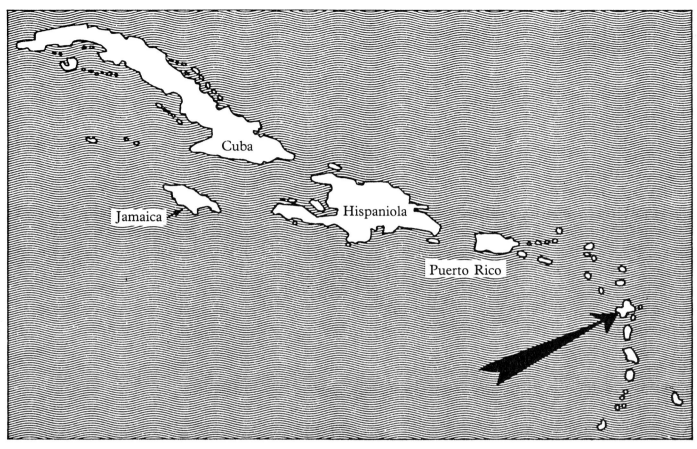

Violet Macaw *(Anodorhynchus purpurascens)*

Way of Life. Although the range of the Hyacinth Macaw covers an area of about 1.5 million km², more than six times greater than the land area of the Federal Republic of Germany, we have only very sparse notes about the life history of these birds. The range of the Hyacinth Macaw covers the midwestern highland region of Brazil as well as a great part of the highlands of the Mato Grosso. The lowlands of the Amazon are not populated by macaws. The Hyacinth Macaw inhabits the gallery forests and somewhat savannahlike areas of riversides and drainage areas of some Amazon, Paraguay, and Paraná tributaries, as well as the riversides southwest of the São Francisco. The meager field reports of this very large parrot species confirm that these macaws appear mainly in pairs. Groups of birds were seldom observed, but, when they were, they were mostly family units of four to five birds.

We tend to think that Hyacinth Macaws are purely virgin-forest birds, and, similarly, we conceive of the Mato Grosso is an impenetrable virgin-forest area. Neither concept is correct. In fact, the habitat of the Hyacinth Macaw is hot, dry scrubland, which is bordered by dry and palm forests only in the vicinity of rivers. Widespread virgin tropical forests do not occur in most of its range; only in the north and the west, adjacent to the range of the Hyacinth Macaw, do the virgin forests, with the diversity we know, begin.

To the south and the northeast the great range of the Hyacinth Macaw abuts the ranges of both related species of the genus: Lear's (*Anodorhynchus leari*) and the Glaucous Macaw (*Anodorhynchus glaucus*). In an impressive report, Prof. Dr. H. Sick discusses Lear's Macaw in its native environment, and, among other things, he describes the inaccessibility of the region. Some areas in the range of the Hyacinth Macaw are probably similar in character.

Brazil

Bolivia

Hyacinth Macaw
(Anodorhynchus hyacinthinus)

The macaws appear to be most numerous in the marshy area of Paraguay, the so-called *pantanal* (which means something like "swamp-prairie") located in the border region of Bolivia and Paraguay. The eastern section of this swamp of vast size offers the Hyacinth Macaws a completely untouched, natural landscape. Exploitation of this region by man is not to be feared, since agriculture or cattle ranching is out of the question. Thus, hope remains that the *pantanal* will remain an intact habitat in the future. Recently, efforts have been made to keep the eastern *pantanal,* which becomes completely marshy during the rainy season beginning in October, dry by means of dams and to use it for raising livestock. The marshes of the Paraguayan lowlands are one of the most unexplored regions of all of South America. It is conceivable that in their forays the Hyacinth Macaws push into the border areas of Bolivia and possibly even Paraguay, because the same environmental conditions are encountered here as in the eastern part of the *pantanal.*

The various palm fruits are the most important dietary staple of the Hyacinth Macaw. The hardest of nutshells offer little resistance to the powerful macaw beaks. Berries, fruits, and buds are eaten in addition to nuts. The course of their day and the rhythm of life is much the same for them as for other macaws. They probably spend the night in small groups, roosting in trees which have long been used for sleeping.

In the morning the birds fly in pairs or in very small parties to the food trees. During the flight, loud, piercing cries are emitted. Despite the slow beat of their wings, which are raised hardly higher than their bodies, flight is swift and looks impressive. Pairs fly close to one another and may be recognized in this way. After the macaws have reached the feeding site, they sit quietly in the treetops to eat in complete peace. Meanwhile, they devote themselves intently to plumage care, so that the feathers of their mate are as carefully groomed as their own. Mutual preening has an important social function and at the same time expresses the pair bond. In the late afternoon hours a communal return flight to the sleeping trees takes place. Hyacinth Macaws do not form groups with other large *Ara* species.

At breeding time, pairs separate from the group and devote themselves to the business of breeding, which takes more than six months, from courtship to complete independence of the young. The female lays up to three eggs, which are incubated for approximately twenty-eight days. Augusto Ruschi reports that the eggs of Hyacinth Macaws are about 53 x 37 mm. and weigh approximately 45 grams. These macaws prefer to nest in the trunks of buriti palms. Incubation of the eggs as well as care of the young birds during the first few weeks of life is done solely by the female. During this time the male keeps watch in the immediate vicinity of the nest cavity. Though the young chicks will leave the nest, which is usually situated at a great height, at the age of about 100 days, the parents still assist them for quite a long while afterward.

P. Roth has made interesting observations of the Hyacinth Macaw. He personally reported to the author that

in August 1976, I encountered the Hyacinth Macaw on an excursion with Dr. Sick in the interior of northern Bahia. In that region, open savannalike *cerrado* vegetation predominates, with groves of buriti palms scattered in moister locations. In these groves we could more or less regularly observe groups of two to eight Hyacinth Macaws. Pairs and families can be recognized in flight by their formations: 2 + 3 + 3, or 2 + 2, or 2 + 1. When we arrived at a palm grove, the birds would fly around us two or three times with loud screams and would come quite close. Then their interest would wane and they would fly away, but normally they would remain within the same buriti grove. With low backlighting or at a great distance the macaws look practically black, hence their local name, *arara preta.*

On August 25, 1976, we discovered a hole in the rocks of the sierra which was occupied by a pair of macaws. As we came into the vicinity of the hole, both macaws repeatedly made patrol flights and settled on the rocky outcroppings of the sierra. As the rock in the area of the hole was friable, we did not succeed in reaching it. As we were departing, it was not long before one macaw flew back into the hole and disappeared (we were barely 100 meters away). Shortly after, the second macaw flew near the hole and then back to an "observation post" to observe us. It sat there for a long time, while the other stayed in the hole. It is likely that this pair had eggs or small chicks there, since their urge to return to it was very strong.

On August 27, 1976, two macaws flew around in front of the rocks of the sierra, calling and perching at various places on the rocks. They finally moved to a white-spotted area which seemed to serve as a "saltlick" for them.

On September 15, 1979, at 12:20 p.m., four Hyacinth Macaws were observed in the *pantanal* near Poconé as they flew over a street and then perched on fence posts. From there, they went to a pond where (as well as I could observe with my telescope) I saw them pull out snails, the same species of snail that also serves the Limpkin (*Aramus guarauna*) as food. Then they perched again on the posts and ate the snails. At times, they would also take the snails up to a nearby tree to eat. They stayed in the tree for about twenty minutes, calling back and forth. (They perched at a height of 4–6 m. in the 12-meter-high tree.) At 2 p.m. they once more flew back over the street.

Care and Breeding. Hyacinth Macaws are the dream of every parrot fancier. Even laymen who see these dark hyacinth blue birds for the first time are greatly impressed by the color of the plumage and the imposing beak. With a size of about 100 cm., Hyacinth Macaws are the largest parrots. Fully grown birds can attain a weight of 2 kg. Nothing can resist the tremendous strength of their powerful beaks. Ordinary commercial parrot cages which would be perfectly suitable for housing other macaws are destroyed by Hyacinths in a very short time. They press the spot-welded wire mesh together with such force that the welds break apart. It is a mere trifle for Hyacinths to effortlessly open brazil nuts, which have a very hard shell. At one importer's, the author was once able to marvel at twelve magnificent Hyacinth Macaws. The birds had completely destroyed their enclosures, massively built parrot cages, and thus were able to more closely investigate the wall of the quarantine station. They gnawed the tiles out of their bed of mortar and even damaged the concrete wall beneath, so that in some places the iron reinforcements were exposed. It should be noted that the animals were under the official import quarantine, and therefore it was impossible to give them branches or tree limbs to gnaw.

Until recently, Hyacinth Macaws were rarely kept by fanciers. Only a few well-known bird and animal parks could show single animals to visitors to their grounds. Recently, Hyacinth Macaws have more often been offered for sale. Their price is relatively high but still favorable, compared to the prices of the large Australian parrots. Hyacinth Macaws

offered for sale in Germany all come from animal dealers in Bolivia and Paraguay. Since the birds do not normally occur in Paraguay or Bolivia (except for some small flocks which occasionally reach the Paraguayan swamp area near the border regions of the two countries) but are indigenous to Brazil, one must ask how the birds came to be in these countries.

In the future it will no longer be possible to import Hyacinth Macaws from South America, because the authorities in Paraguay and Bolivia cannot provide the official export and import documents which the German Federal Republic demands in accordance with the Washington Convention (CITES). It is said that in a few years Hyacinth Macaws will disappear from the fancy unless specialists discover how to propagate these birds. Parrot lovers who have single birds should consider obtaining mates for them or loaning a single bird to a breeder. Only in this way will it be possible in the future to maintain a small population of Hyacinth Macaws in captivity.

The Hyacinth Macaw is a bird that tames quickly and forms an intimate relationship with its owner. Under normal circumstances it will not bite; a stranger, however, should always be careful in dealing with such a bird and never tease or corner it, for it could use its powerful beak for defense and possibly bite off a finger.

The first successful breeding of a Hyacinth Macaw is said to have taken place at the zoo in Kobe, Japan, in 1968. The *International Zoo Yearbook* reported the successful rearing of one youngster. The first successful European breeding took place in the Bratislava zoo in Czechoslovakia; three chicks were raised by the parents (a confirmation of this breeding has not been submitted; possibly it was in fact *Ara ararauna*).

At Brookfield Park, Illinois, a Hyacinth Macaw female laid two eggs in March 1969. They were not fertile. Two months later, egg laying resumed, and on May 13 and May 16 each, an egg was laid. On June 13, a chick emerged, but, unfortunately, it died three days later. In 1970, the Hyacinth Macaw pair were put in an indoor flight measuring 2.0 x 4.0 x 1.5 meters. The nest box, a 50-gallon barrel, was the same one used for nesting in the previous breeding season. The flight was kept at a high temperature with high humidity. On January 5 and 9, 1971, eggs were once again laid, but again they were infertile. More eggs were laid on March 1 and 4, and after an incubation period of twenty-nine days, one chick emerged from the egg laid on March 1. Unfortunately, the female did not tend the chick. In April 1971, a single egg was laid. In the beginning of December, two more eggs were laid. On January 4, a chick emerged, weighing 18.6 grams. The young bird was fed by the parents until it was forty-one days old, by which time it had attained a weight of 643 grams. The hen was plucking the youngster, so it was decided to hand-rear it.

By March 1972, it was again time for egg laying, although once more the eggs were infertile. On May 1 and 5, another clutch was laid. On May 29, a chick emerged from the first egg. After July 27, the chick had to be hand-reared because the parents were plucking it and it had become encrusted with food remnants. In May, October, and December of 1973, additional chicks were born. All of them were reared by hand.

Although the Hyacinth Macaw pair in the Brookfield Zoo were always eager to breed and regularly produced eggs, almost every time the parents failed in rearing. As a rule, with nearly every species of macaw, the first clutch is either unsuccessful or very problematical; but from the second brood, the difficulties in courting, incubating, and rearing decrease, for the most part. Thus the pair of Hyacinth Macaws in the Brookfield Zoo are, in respect to rearing young, a notable exception.

Hyacinth Macaws have been kept for many years in the bird park at Walsrode, Germany, the largest such park in the world. The male macaw showed a remarkable reaction following the sudden death of his mate. The macaws were housed in the indoor flight with an area of 6.0 + 2.5 m., and 2.5 m. high. For many days courtship behavior, attempts at copulation, and nest-box investigation, along with the usual frequent cries and jerky head movements, were observed. Whenever the keeper came within sight of the pair, he would be greeted with loud screeching.

One morning, for no apparent reason, the female lay dead on the ground. The behavior of the male toward his dead mate was fascinating. He ran around the female screeching; calling softly, he tried, without touching her, to cajole her with attraction calls into standing up. By morning feeding time, when the sorry state of affairs was confirmed, the male had already tramped a path in the sand around the female by his persistent running around. This behavior was shown only when the male thought he was not being observed. When the keeper approached, the bird was openly aggressive and tried to defend the female. Because of this behavior, the dead bird was not removed for some hours. Until that time, the male continued the reactions described above at the same level of intensity. After removal of the female, which was the external releasing factor, the male's behavior abruptly changed. He immediately relaxed and was thereafter unobtrusive. A little later he took food. Three months later it was possible to supply the male with a new hen. Both birds were perfectly compatible, and it was soon time for egg laying. In the case of the female, and only with the female, the color of the bare facial skin changed a few days before laying eggs. The yellow orange skin color became a pale yellow. Possibly, alteration of the bare facial skin is a sex-specific characteristic which appears during the breeding period.

Additional successful Hyacinth Macaw breedings occurred at the Houston Zoo in the United States. Already in 1972, this zoo had an extremely impressive parrot breeding with the successful rearing of the rare St. Vincent Amazon (*Amazona guildingii*). In 1975 the breeding of a Hyacinth Macaw could also be announced. Hybrids have occurred between the Hyacinth and the Blue-and-yellow Macaw (*Ara ararauna*) and the Hyacinth and the Scarlet Macaw (*Ara macao*). Both hybrids occurred in Salt Lake City in the United States.

Glaucous Macaw
Anodorhynchus glaucus
(Vieillot 1816)

Characteristics. Size, about 72 cm. Greenish blue. Throat and cheeks as well as the upper breast have a trace of brownish gray. Belly greenish blue. Underside of tail feathers brownish black. Bare eye ring and bare skin beside the base of the lower mandible yellow. Iris dark brown. Beak black, somewhat lighter toward the tip. Feet dark brownish black. Female probably like the male. Young birds probably like adults.

Range. Central and southern Paraguay. Extreme southwestern Mato Grosso in Brazil. Northeastern Argentina. Possibly also northwestern Uruguay and western Rio Grande do Sul in Brazil.

Way of Life. The Glaucous Macaw is an extremely rare bird that lives primarily along the Paraguay and west of the Paraná rivers. The landscapes in this almost unsettled region are very diverse. (About eighty percent of the entire population of 2.8 million live in the environs of the capital city, Asunción.) One finds that east of the Paraguayan lowlands, the terrain is hill country, covered with rainforest, 200 to 600 m. in altitude. The watercourses, often extensive swamp areas devoid of people, are bordered by open grasslands and forests and often resemble parkland. The Paraguay itself floods with high water to a distance of 40 km. To the west is the Gran Chaco, which gradually rises westward, with dry forest and thornbush. The climate is characterized by the change from the subtropical to the tropical zones. In northeastern Argentina and northwestern Uruguay, one finds temperate-zone climate.

As mentioned previously, the Glaucous Macaw principally dwells in the great flood plain of the Paraguay and its river tributaries. Since these regions are partly inaccessible, it is understandable that these macaws can be observed only in small numbers. The meager details about the life of the Glaucous Macaw in the wild give rise to the suspicion that the birds lead a highly nomadic life and only during the breeding season linger in one place for any length of time. Northwestern Uruguay and the western part of Rio Grande do Sul (Brazil) are or have been visited by macaws only in the "quest for food" outside the breeding season.

Information concerning nesting habits is not available. However, it may be assumed that, like other parrot species found in this area, the Glaucous Macaw begins to breed in October. The nestling period concludes in January or February.

Some ornithologists firmly hold the opinion that the Glaucous Macaw is already extinct. The "searches" of past years have been unproductive; hence, this conjecture suggests itself. The author believes that such judgements are sometimes made too soon and that often the designation "extinct" is a sham. Some instances from the recent past show that various animal species which had been declared extinct suddenly reappeared. In the late autumn of 1982, the author received a report that a Bolivian animal dealer had obtained live Glaucous Macaws. No confirmation was ever received, but, as incredible as the announcement may seem at first, it is really not all that incredible. For example, some specialists believed that Lear's Macaw (*Anodorhynchus leari*) was an extinct species, although time and again single specimens appeared in the trade. It took years before Prof. Dr. Sick produced official proof of the separate status and the population size of Lear's Macaw. A similar situation could occur with the Glaucous Macaw.

Care and Breeding. Currently the Glaucous Macaw is not found either in zoos or in the possession of fanciers. During the last century, single specimens were exhibited in London, Amsterdam, and Berlin. A Glaucous Macaw, supposedly, was kept for some years in Australia, probably around 1960. In the opinion of the author, the facts indicate that the Glaucous Macaw is an absolute rarity. It appears that this macaw, besides the pygmy-parrots (*Micropsitta*) and the Blue-headed Macaw (*Ara couloni*), is the only living parrot species that is not kept in captivity. Of course, it is possible that a Glaucous Macaw may not be recognized as such by those who own one.

The author remembers visiting an animal dealer several years ago; among other specimens, he was shown two blue macaws. At this time the Hyacinth Macaw was extremely rare and very seldom encountered in the bird trade. In retrospect, I believe that both of these birds were Glaucous Macaws. For one thing, their color was more a sea blue, and both were noticeably smaller than full-grown Hyacinth Macaws. In addition, in shape the head and beak were not so massive, and the bare skin at the base of the beak and around the eye was a more citron yellow color. I then tried to follow the trail of these macaws, but unfortunately that was no longer possible. There is a definite possibility that some individuals among the imported blue macaws are not recognized as

A. F. Lydon prepared this illustration of the Hyacinth
Macaw for Dr. Greene's *Parrots in Captivity.*

49

Glaucous Macaw
(Anodorhynchus glaucus)

Glaucous Macaws and are thought to be young Hyacinth Macaws.

There was a Glaucous Macaw on exibit in a Dutch or Belgian bird park in the late 1970s.

In 1928, Haberlandt of Magdeburg reported on a visit to a Dutch animal dealer, named Blazer, in Rotterdam. At the time, this was one of the greatest specialty shops of its kind. Among other things, it employed six animal collectors in various parts of the world. In his visit Haberlandt was able to see, besides the Hyacinth Macaw (*Anodorhynchus hyacinthinus*), some specimens of Lear's Macaw (*A. leari*) and the Glaucous Macaw.

The Glaucous Macaw, a very rare species in its range, is included in Appendix I of the Washington Convention and therefore may be traded commercially only with special governmental permission.

Lear's Macaw
Anodorhynchus leari
Bonaparte 1856

Characteristics. Size, about 75 cm. Dark blue. Head, neck, and underside more greenish gray blue. Back, wings, and tail cobalt blue. Underside of tail dark gray blue. Iris, dark brown. Bare eye ring and skin beside the base of the lower mandible, yellowish. Beak black. Toes gray black. Female probably like the male. Young birds probably like adults.

Range. Eastern Brazil, in the provinces of Pernambuco and Bahia; possibly the range is even more extensive.

Remarks. The Prince of Canino and Musignano, Charles Lucien Jules Laurent Bonaparte (1803–1857), in 1856 named this macaw in honor of the English bird painter Edward Lear (1812–1888).

For years there was doubt as to whether Lear's Macaw was a separate species. Some ornithologists surmised that Lear's Macaw, based on its rarity and its appearance, was a hybrid between the Hyacinth Macaw (*Anodorhynchus hyacinthinus*) and the Glaucous Macaw (*Anodorhynchus glaucus*). This

could not be proved, however, and in view of the distribution of the Glaucous Macaw it seemed extremely doubtful. That Lear's Macaw is a distinct species was confirmed only in 1978, when Prof. Dr. H. Sick found the area to which it is endemic.

Way of Life. Lear's Macaw is one of the rarest parrots in existence; however, it is questionable whether it is really as rare as some "Caribe" amazons; for example, the Imperial Amazon (*Amazona imperialis*), the St. Vincent Amazon (*Amazona guildingii*), the St. Lucia Amazon (*Amazona versicolor*), the Red-necked Amazon (*Amazona arausiaca*), or even as rare as the Puerto Rican Amazon (*Amazona vittata vittata*), which has a population of about fifty animals.

Even at the present time the range of Lear's Macaw is as good as unexplored, and therefore we can surmise that this species is more numerous in the wild than was once supposed. Prof. Dr. Sick of the University of Rio de Janeiro—who is also associated with the natural history museum there—actually produced proof in 1978 that Lear's Macaw is a separate species. Dr. Sick wrote the following letter to Dr. J. Steinbacher, editor of the specialist journal *Die Gefiederte Welt*:

I have succeeded in solving the greatest mystery in the ornithology of South America—not only Brazil—by finding the home of Lear's Macaw, a splendid, great, blue bird (74 cm. in overall length) which, until now, was only known in the captive state. I had previously searched in vain twice before, but this time I came to precisely the right spot, the Raso da Catarina in northern Bahia, which, in my estimation, is the last place left where this bird could still hide. Since 1856, scientists have been wracking their brains over this problem. As it was impossible to find the bird in the wild, before long one of the best contemporary ornithologists, a Dutchman, put forth the theory that it was really not a species. Still, some specimens occasionally appeared in the animal trade (very seldom; in September 1977, I made a special flight from San Francisco to San Diego, where the famous zoo had a pair; also, Walsrode has or had Lear's Macaw)—these he explained as hybrids of two other long-known species. This appeared quite clever, but I had not the smallest doubt that this was not the case; it was the idea of a museum man, someone unfamiliar with live birds.

I brought back with me a fine, carefully prepared specimen, the first to come to a museum (Rio) after being collected in the wild. We saw as many as twenty-one

1 ▲

2 ◀

3 ◀

1. Intact coastal virgin tropical forest may be found in only a few areas of Middle and South America. Human settlement usually began on the coast; very soon, destructive incursions into the backcountry started, and the native flora and fauna had to give way. 2. This nesting tree in the northern Gran Chaco region emerges noticeably from the surrounding vegetation. Macaws take the choice nest sites in free-standing, dead trees. 3. In highland regions where bare rock is exposed, macaws often use the crevices and holes for nesting.

1. In many macaw species, a characteristic of a young bird is the brownish color of the iris, which is clearly evident in this Blue-and-yellow Macaw *(Ara ararauna)*. **2.** Although the Blue-and-yellow Macaw does not exhibit geographic races, local color variations are found. **3.** According to the photographer's identification, this photograph shows a Lear's Macaw *(Anodorhynchus leari)*. Yet the coloration of this animal as it appears here suggests instead a Glaucous Macaw *(Anodorhynchus glaucus)*, for Lear's Macaw has a greater amount of blue in its plumage. **4.** This Blue-and-yellow Macaw produces a pigment that makes the feathers take on a brownish black color instead of blue.

individuals flying together and found roosting and nesting sites in inaccessible cavities in the rocks of deeply cut, canyonlike dry river valleys. It is the only macaw species that occurs there.

The journey was not easy, even for a healthy man and young people (my assistants are 20 and 21 years old). We took endless rides on pack animals; as they were without saddles, we sat instead on a wooden frame for hanging packs, which did not have stirrups. Our dangling legs were without support and would "fall asleep" from the pressure on the blood vessels of the thighs. On one of the first days of the trip, I had an attack of malaria. My assistants often had fevers, diarrhea, sunburn, and wounds from plants, etc. For them the trip was a fabulous adventure; even I, in a sense, enjoyed it, but for me it was more deadly serious. After one hours-long night march (our guide had got lost) in very deep, loose sand through the trackless thornbush *caatinga*, I was so close to exhaustion that I thought that it all could end, now that the great victory had been achieved. We mostly ruined my Toyota-Mercedes-Deisel four-wheel drive, the strongest truck there is in Brazil, in the roadless Raso da Catarina, but it didn't matter; I had bought it for the purpose, and the great result was there. Finally, we had to leave the Toyota behind and to continue in the trailer of a tractor I had rented from a government agency at the border of the region. We either rode or ran along; but too often the tractor would get stuck, and we would have to laboriously dig it out again.

The Raso da Catarina is one of the most inaccessible regions of Brazil, notorious for the Canudos War of 1897 and the subsequent hunt for the bandit Lampiao. Brazil received all of its war materiel from Germany, so we found a German army pistol. Even Krupp cannons were hauled into the *caatinga*, where they proved to be totally useless. (In the early 1930s a Brazilian film, *O Cangaceiro*, dealing with this material was awarded a prize in Berlin.) In the Canudos War, the revolt of a very small group of religious fanatics against the republic, more than a thousand soldiers, elite troops from Rio, São Paulo, etc., were lost; it is said that most died of thirst. We had sixty liters of water with us, which forced us to use it extremely sparingly (with four or five guides).

My hope of finding completely unknown birds in the range of Lear's Macaw has not been fulfilled. The most interesting species was an ovenbird (family Furnariidae) that lives hidden on the ground, but unfortunately, though rare, it was already known from areas nearby. Through my incredible knowledge of bird calls, I am able to locate a bird immediately, even if it persists in hiding, and these tend to be the most interesting. The call of the ovenbird was the only one in that area unknown to me. This technique is not always applicable,

for example, with hummingbirds, which are common in the Raso. We are developing a program for another visit to the area, and perhaps we can get a helicopter from the government.

The first announcement about the finding of Lear's Macaw will appear in *Alauda* (France). The editor, Jacques Vielliard, who accompanied me on my first quest for Lear's Macaw and is now back in Brazil, can help me to have it published as quickly as possible.

At the end of the macaw program (one and a half months), I realized I was not up to the second part of the journey (another month and a half working on extremely rare cracids in Alagoas, a state neighboring Bahia, which I had reported about at the Berlin [Ornithological] Congress). In the meantime, we had reached Recife (Pernambuco).

P.S.: Raso—during the hottest hours, even my companions were often not inclined to run around. We looked for a little shade and lay in the sand or on the stones without moving.

On my sixty-ninth birthday, January 10, I sat in one of the macaw canyons and observed at least fifteen of the animals arriving to sleep. I used my new large telescope, which was delivered to me by the Brazilian research service a few days before my departure for Bahia. It was imported from East-Zeiss after a year-long battle. The field of view precisely encompassed a pair of the proud birds (minus the long tails). They were surrounded by a thick swarm of flies and often scratched their heads nervously. It was truly the most memorable birthday of my life!

Dr. H. Sick reported on his work at the first Ibero-American Ornithological Congress in Buenos Aires, Argentina, and he received the Gold Medal of Brazil for his discovery of the place of origin of Lear's Macaw.

One Lear's Macaw exhibited by the municipality of Santo Antão (Pernambuco) is said to have been captured in the vicinity of Juàzeiro, a small city on the left bank of the São Francisco (a river which separates Pernambuco and Bahia). Otherwise, no field observations about Lear's Macaws have been noted. No reports have been made concerning its breeding habits. It is to be assumed that the range of these macaws is known only to a few natives and that the birds often shown in zoological gardens are there only by chance.

Care and Breeding. As we have learned, Lear's Macaw is an extremely rare bird. Individual

Lear's Macaw
(Anodorhynchus leari)

The larger macaws, because of their splendid colors and size, are often the most conspicuous birds on exhibit at bird parks. The Walsrode collection includes this Military Macaw *(Ara militaris)*.

1. Spix's Macaw *(Cyanopsitta spixii)* is one of the rarest of parrots. In recent years, the bird park at Walsrode is the only place where it has been exhibited to the public. Spix's Macaw is the sole member of the genus *Cyanopsitta*. 2. The Blue-and-yellow Macaw *(Ara ararauna)* is the species most favored by bird fanciers and breeders. 3. A Hyacinth Macaw pair. 4. Like all other macaw species, Hyacinth Macaws *(Anodorhynchus hyacinthinus)* should generally be kept in spacious aviaries. Only in such accommodations can these animals flourish and exhibit their impressive flying ability.

specimens came by chance to North America and Europe. Years ago, when parrots could still be exported from Brazil (the Brazilian government has by now had a general trade prohibition for years), very occasionally Lear's Macaws, mixed in with Hyacinth Macaws *(Anodorhynchus hyacinthinus)*, managed to get to European or North American zoos. During the last century, single specimens were exhibited in the London Zoo, including even an egg (57.0 x 38.4 mm.), which today may be found in the collection of the British Museum of National History. In recent years, for the most part only single animals could be seen only in the zoological gardens in San Diego, Los Angeles, and Brookfield in the United States, as well as in Copenhagen, Basel, and Walsrode. Whether Lear's Macaws exist in private collections is questionable; if they do, it would be deplorable.

A pair of Lear's Macaws is supposed to have bred successfully a few years ago at the zoological gardens in Basel. However, the young bird died before the nestling period was over. In the meantime, one of the parent birds also died, so that now only one specimen of this rare species is present in Basel.

T. Silva (pers. comm.) informed the author that in 1982, Busch Gardens in Tampa, Florida, in cooperation with Parrot Jungle, was successful in achieving offspring from Lear's Macaw. Parrot Jungle in Miami, which owns a single male, placed it at the disposal of Busch Gardens, where a female was available. The two macaws were introduced successfully, and one chick resulted. In order to afford the baby bird the greatest possible chance for survival, it was immediately sent to Parrot Jungle in Miami for hand-rearing. Parrot Jungle had, in previous years, achieved good results in hand-rearing other macaw species, and they were equally successful with this rare specimen. In September 1982, a second chick hatched. The offspring remained with the parent birds, then approximately 30 years old, and they reared the chick without problems.

Dr. J. M. Lernould, director of the zoological and botanical park in Mulhous, France, has told the author that there are probably two Lear's Macaws in France. One is said to be in the Ménagerie in Paris, while the second is privately owned.

Lear's Macaw is listed in Appendix I of the Washington Convention (CITES).

In September 1929, a male Lear's Macaw from the Frankfurt zoo was deposited in the Senckenberg research institute and natural-history museum in Frankfurt. The bird had probably been exhibited as *Anodorhynchus glaucus* (Glaucous Macaw) in the Frankfurt zoo, because it was originally labeled as such.

Genus *CYANOPSITTA* Bonaparte 1854

The genus *Cyanopsitta* shows a very close relationship to the genus *Anodorhynchus*. The genus consists of only Spix's Macaw, a species of medium size. The genus-specific characteristics are the unfeathered eye ring and the bare loral region. The unfeathered areas make the dark gray skin visible. The plumage color is uniformly blue to gray. There are no sex-specific characteristics by which one can differentiate male and female birds, nor are there recognizable differences between young and adult birds. The genus *Cyanopsitta* may be considered intermediate between *Anodorhynchus* and *Ara*.

Spix's Macaw *Cyanopsitta spixii* (Wagler 1832)

Characteristics. Size, about 56 cm. Dark cobalt blue. Head, cheeks, and ear region gray blue, becoming grayish green blue on the nape and breast. Bare skin area from the lores to the eye gray. Underside of tail feathers dark gray. Iris light gray. Beak black. Feet grayish black. Female probably like the male. Young birds probably like adults.

Range. Brazil: Southern Piaui, western Pernambuco, northern Bahia, and possibly southernmost Maranhao.

Remarks. Johann George Wagler (1800–1832), who at an early age became a professor of zoology

Spix's Macaw
(Cyanopsitta spixii)

Brazil

Of these watercolors from Rothschild's *Extinct Birds,* all but *Ara tricolor* were prepared from the reports and drawings of traveling naturalists, traders, and colonists. These macaws were island dwellers of the Greater and Lesser Antilles; Their existence cannot be proven a hundred percent even now. 1. *Anodorhynchus purpurascens* (Violet Macaw) from Gradeloupe, W.I. 2. *Ara erythrura* (Mysterious Macaw) from the West Indies. 3. *Ara tricolor* (Cuban Macaw). Around 1800 this macaw was still relatively common in Cuba. The rapid settlement and heavy agricultural exploitation of the island led to the extirpation of the species in a very short time. 4. *Ara erythrocephala* (Green-and-yellow Macaw) from Jamaica.

1. *Ara gossei* (Yellow-headed Macaw) from Jamaica. **2.** *Ara martinica* (Orange-bellied Macaw). **3.** This watercolor painted from museum specimens by Thomas Arndt shows on the left the Glaucous Macaw *(Anodorhynchus glaucus),* which some ornithologists suspect is extinct. On the right is Lear's Macaw *(Anodorhychus leari).* The color of Lear's Macaw is quite similar to that of the Hyacinth Macaw, although Lear's is a markedly smaller bird, and the bare yellow skin around the lower mandible is disposed differently. **4.** The Blue-headed Macaw *(Ara couloni).* This illustration by Thomas Arndt is a true-color rendering of a skin in the Senckenberg museum in Frankfurt.

at the university in Munich, shortly before his death named this small dark blue macaw after its discoverer, Dr. Johannes Baptist von Spix (1781–1826): *Sittace spixii*. With the botanist Dr. C. E. P. Martius, Spix traveled through parts of Brazil from 1817 to 1820 and there found Spix's Macaw. He returned to Munich with a great collection of specimens for the museum.

Way of Life. Spix's Macaw lives in the northern highlands of Brazil. The climate of this country is tropical, and precipitation is irregular, with long dry periods. The vegetation in the *caatinga*, a dry region, has adapted to the sparse precipitation, which produces a meager scrub landscape. Small gallery forests and swampy woodlands are found in the vicinity of rivers. Opening this region to agriculture did not prove to be advantageous for raising crops or for breeding cattle; therefore after brief attempts they were allowed to lapse. Thus, the *caatinga* appears essentially undisturbed, providing an intact living space for Spix's Macaw. Though ideal living conditions still exist, it is a rare species in its range. In the wild, Spix's Macaw is just as uncommon as the three blue macaw species related to it, especially the Glaucous Macaw (*Anodorhynchus glaucus*) and Lear's Macaw (*Anodorhynchus leari*). The author believes that in the *caatinga* nature limits the populations of some species by means of the extreme climatic conditions. The Yellow-faced Amazon (*Amazona xanthops*), which lives in the same biotope, is also extremely rare and confirms the thesis that a wide variety of species occur in the *caatinga*, but that any given species will be present only in small numbers. Spix's Macaws live in open bush country interspersed with gallery forests. They maintain a very great fleeing distance, so they are usually observed only by accident.

No actual details are available about the breeding season, but it could begin in December and last about four months until the young are fledged. It is also conceivable that Spix's Macaws time their breeding to coincide with the variable periods of precipitation and that the birds start to breed during the period of most favorable plant growth. An egg in the British Museum of Natural History measures 34.9 x 28.7 mm.

Care and Breeding. Since Spix's Macaw is listed in the appendix of the Washington Convention (CITES) and, consequently, also in the appendix of the Federal Republic of Germany's species-protection ordinance, it may be traded commercially only with a special official permit.

It has been possible for very few bird fanciers to keep the rare Spix's Macaw, and only a few bird and animal parks have been able to exhibit the birds. The first Spix's Macaws arrived at the Berlin Zoo in 1893. Currently, Spix's Macaws can be found in some American and European bird parks, such as, for example, Walsrode, where a single bird is on exhibit (although formerly there were two specimens), and the Naples Zoo. The zoo in Rio de Janeiro always provides a rewarding visit for parrot fanciers with its varied stock of native parrots; two Spix's Macaws can be seen in Rio. Dr. H. Strunden (1974) comments on these two birds: "In the large enclosure both birds were very animated and exhibited a wide assortment of behaviors. These ranged from reciprocal preening to violent fighting, with the weaker bird finally lying on its back on the ground, although it knew how to defend its skin and feathers with its beak, feet, and loud screaming."

In 1975, the bird park at Walsrode was able to acquire two young Spix's Macaws. When it appeared that they might actually be a pair of this extremely rare species, hope for eventual progeny arose. Unfortunately, the cock died in 1978, and the hope was dashed. The singly kept female remaining in the bird park, in flawless plumage, is a pleasing representative of the species. The bird is never bored, as she busies herself the entire day with intense feather care, observing the parrots in the neighboring flight and diligently gnawing branches and limbs. In 1981, after much effort, the bird park succeeded in obtaining a male for breeding purposes from Dr. G. A. Smith of England. Unfortunately, the male is physically impaired, but, nevertheless, it is hoped that the animals will be compatible and, if at all possible, there will be offspring in the near future.

The director of the avian section of the Naples Zoo, Frau Wenner, told the author that a pair of this rare species is housed in the bird area in an outdoor flight with a masonry shelter. The female has been at the zoo since 1954, the male since 1974.

Dominican Macaw *(Ara atwoodi)*

The flight has a total area of 4.3 x 1.2 m. and a height of about 1.7 m. Of the two nest boxes made available, the one standing on the ground in the shelter was chosen. This box (35 x 35 x 45 cm.) had a layer of peat strewn in it. On the peat the birds placed small stones which they carried in themselves. When Frau Wenner was in Brazil several years ago, people familiar with the area inhabited by Spix's Macaw told her that a large part of the region was impassable swamp land. The many dead trees standing in the swamps served Spix's Macaws as nesting sites. Apparently, the macaws place a layer of small stones in the nest hole to provide drainage system for rainwater entering the nest.

It was only in 1980 that the macaw female showed any interest in the male. Previously, she was more attached to a cock Hyacinth Macaw *(Anodorhynchus hyacinthinus)* in a neighboring flight. During the day the large and small blue macaws

hung on the wire mesh and preened each other's feathers. In 1980, egg laying began. The first egg was laid in the nest box. The second egg lay broken under the perch. A short time later the first egg was crushed in the nest box. In 1981, the female again laid two eggs, but these were broken on the layer of stones, just as in the previous year. One hopes things will work out better the next time. It would be nice if they could succeed in having these rare birds produce offspring.

H. H. Jacobsen of Risskov, Denmark, told the author that T. Silva of the United States had been informed about a breeding and rearing of Spix's Macaw at Alvaro Cavalhaes's in the 1960s. Unfortunately, no details about this supposed first captive breeding were kept.

The late president of Yugoslavia, Tito, is supposed to have kept between two and four Spix's Macaws in his private zoo. Furthur details about these animals, however, are not available.

Illiger's Macaw, A. F. Lydon's illustration in *Parrots in Captivity* by W. T. Greene.

St. Croix Macaw *(Ara autocthones)*

In the future, Spix's Macaws will probably be extremely rare guests in the aviaries of bird fanciers and zoological gardens. It is to be feared that the birds will soon disappear from captivity completely.

Genus *ARA* Lacepède 1799

The distinctive characteristic of all species of the genus *Ara* is the bare area of the cheek, beak, and eye region. The extent of the bare area varies greatly, and in some species lines of feathers run through it. The genus includes species which vary in size from about 38 cm. to 90 cm. Nearly all of the species lack sex-specific characteristics, but young birds may often be recognized by the color of the iris. In all, the genus *Ara* consists of twelve living species.

Dominican Macaw *Ara atwoodi* Clarke 1908

Range. Dominica (West Indies)

Remarks. In 1908, Clarke described *Ara atwoodi* after an unconfirmed report by Thomas Atwood (1791). According to Atwood, there lived on Dominica a parrot which was bigger than the normal parrots (probably he is comparing it to *parakeets*) and was colored mainly green and yellow. The head of the bird was said to have red markings. Wing and tail feathers were colored differently from one another. Whether *Ara atwoodi* is actually an endemic representative of the genus *Ara* or possibly an escaped or introduced captive Military Macaw (*Ara militaris*) or Great Green Macaw (*Ara ambigua*) cannot be verified from the extant notes.

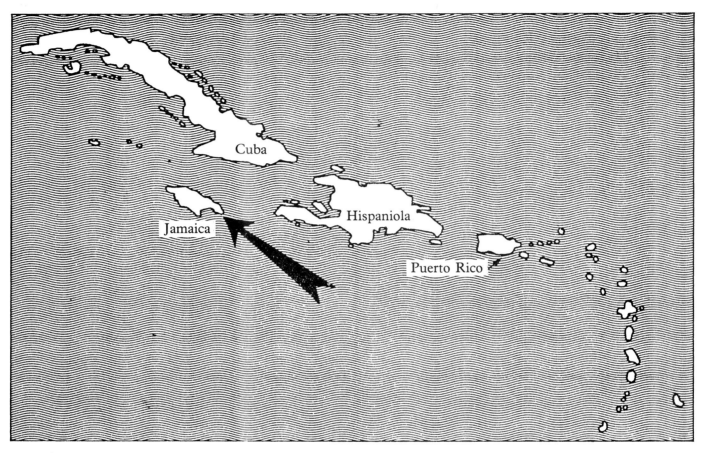

Mysterious Macaw *(Ara erythrura)*

The occurrence of a macaw species on a Caribbean island is not at all unlikely, since a native macaw species (the Cuban Macaw, *Ara tricolor*) once lived on Cuba and the Isle of Pines.

St. Croix Macaw
Ara autocthones
Wetmore 1937

Range. St. Croix (Virgin Islands, West Indies).

Remarks. Skeletal remains of a macaw species is said to have been found in a kitchen midden (Wetmore 1937). It is probably a case of a macaw brought to St. Croix and eaten there. There is no positive evidence of the actual existence of macaws on St. Croix.

Mysterious Macaw
Ara erythrura
Rothschild 1907

Range. West Indies

Remarks. A highly doubtful species; its range is assumed to be the West Indies, and Jamaica in particular. Names for it can be traced in reports back to the seventeenth century (de Rochefort 1658). Possibly this hearsay macaw is identical with the Orange-bellied Macaw (*Ara martinica* Rothschild 1905). In 1906, Prof. Salvadori called Rothschild's attention to an error in his 1905 description, in which the species was given the name *Anodorhynchus coeruleus* Rothschild 1905. In *Extinct Birds* (1907b: 54), Rothschild gave the correct description of this macaw: "The color characters exhibit a very great similarity to *Ara*

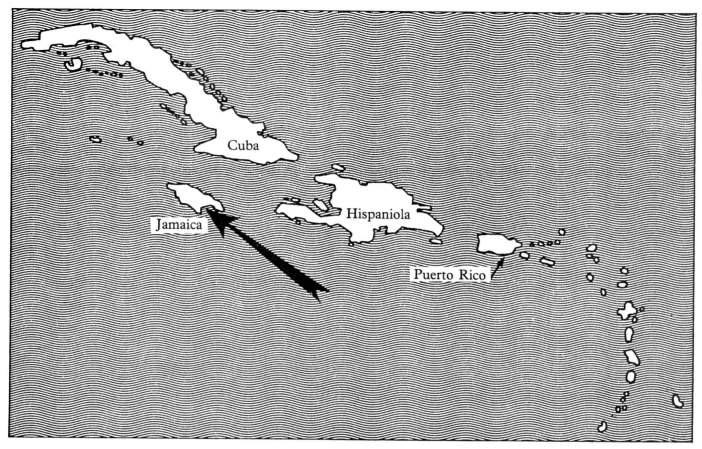

Green-and-yellow Macaw *(Ara erythrocephala)*

araruana." Rothschild adds (p. 53) that on Jamaica, in the vicinity of the harbor of St. James, two large yellow-and-blue macaws were seen by a Mr. Comard. Rothschild believes that these birds are "his" *Ara erythrura* and that its range should be the West Indies.

central range in Jamaica, in a very rainy area, a Mr. Hill saw some macaws which bore a certain similarity to the Great Green and Military macaws (*Ara ambigua* and *Ara militaris*). The birds probably became extinct in the same century. (See Gosse 1847: 261; Rothschild 1905: 14, 1907a: 201.)

Green-and-yellow Macaw
Ara erythrocephala
Rothschild 1905

Range. Jamaica.

Remarks. In the eighteenth century, at St. Ann and Trelawney, at the northernmost foothills of the

Yellow-headed Macaw
Ara gossei
Rothschild 1905

Range. Jamaica

Remarks. The Yellow-headed Macaw, which is also called the "Jamaican" Macaw, is said to have

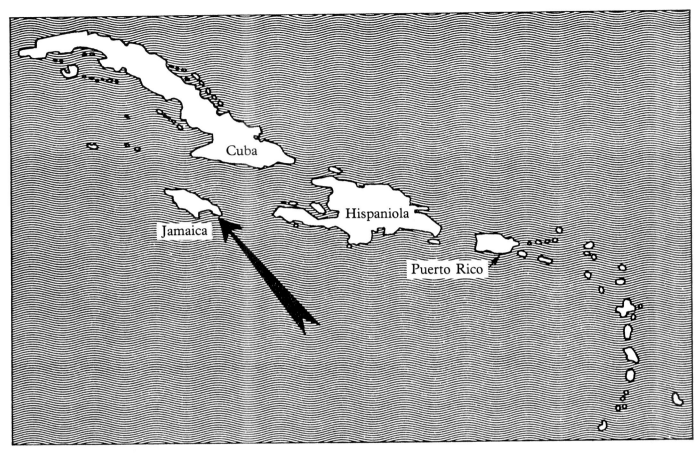

Yellow-headed Macaw *(Ara gossei)*

been very similar to the Cuban Macaw (*Ara tricolor*) from Cuba. The range of *Ara gossei* probably extended to the northwestern part of Jamaica. According to a statement by Gosse (1847: 260), the last Yellow-headed Macaw was shot in 1765 in the vicinity of Lucea.

According to Gosse, *Ara gossei* differs from *Ara tricolor* by virtue of the yellow area on its head. From other depictions, it appears that a macaw similar to *Ara tricolor* at one time lived on Haiti (Hispaniola). It is quite possible that *Ara tricolor* occurred on the islands of Cuba, Jamaica, and Haiti and was composed of island races: (1) *Ara tricolor tricolor*—Cuba and Isle of Pines; (2) *Ara tricolor gossei*—Jamaica; and (3) *Ara tricolor haitius*—Hispaniola. (See also Rothschild 1905: 14, 1907a: 201; Clarke 1905: 348.)

Guadeloupe Red Macaw
Ara guadeloupensis
Clarke 1905

Range. West Indies

Remarks. The *Ara guadeloupensis* described by Clarke in 1905 is said to have lived in the West Indian islands of Guadeloupe, Martinique, and possibly Dominica. Even Columbus in 1496 reported that red parrots were kept by Carib Indians on Martinique. According to the description of du Tertre (1667) the Guadeloupe Red Macaw had a certain resemblance to the Scarlet Macaw (*Ara macao*) and the Cuban Macaw (*Ara tricolor*). In d'Aubenton's book (1779), it is called *Ara rouge*. Probably the Guadeloupe Red Macaw was already extinct or had been extirpated by the beginning of the eighteenth century.

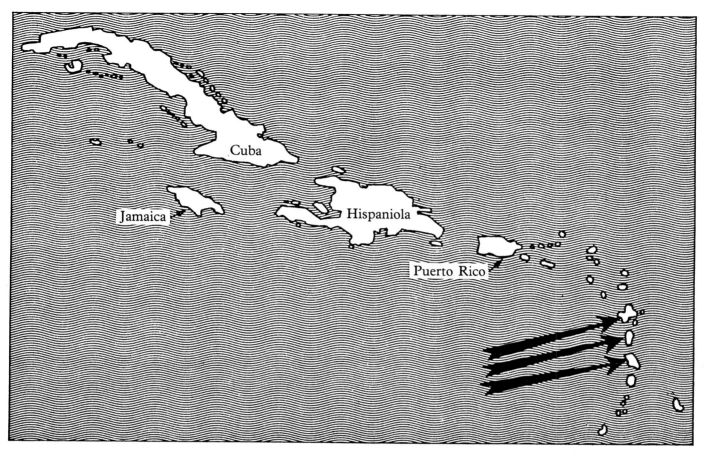

Guadeloupe Red Macaw *(Ara guadeloupensis)*

Orange-bellied Macaw
Ara martinica
(Rothschild 1905)

Range. Martinique

Remarks. The description of the Orange-bellied Macaw rests on a very old description from an earlier century (Bouton 1635). Here it will be treated as a species that can be seen to be very closely related to the Blue-and-yellow Macaw (*Ara ararauna*), from the evidence of Père Bouton. It is likely that the animal became extinct in the seventeenth century. (See Rothschild 1905: 14, 1907a: 202, 1907b: 53.)

Cuban Macaw
Ara tricolor
Bechstein 1811

Range. Central and western Cuba; Isle of Pines.

Characteristics. Size, ca. 45–50 cm. Scarlet red. Under parts darker red. Crown yellowish red. Nape yellow. Upper back cinnamon red, edged with green. Rump and upper tail coverts, light blue. Wings, purple blue. Lesser wing coverts blue, edged with brownish red. Tail feathers red brown, red toward the base, blue toward the tip. Small bare area extending from around the eyes to the beak marked with a few feathers, red and black. Beak black gray. Feet grayish.

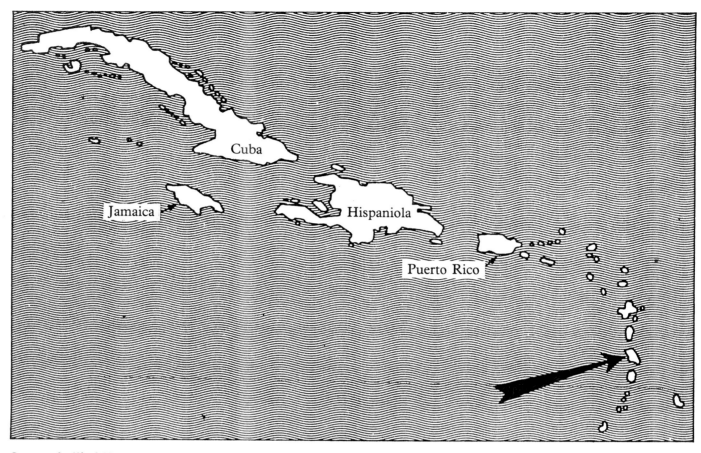

Orange-bellied Macaw *(Ara martinica)*

Way of Life. Only the most meager information about the behavior of the Cuban Macaw is extant. Around 1850 only a few specimens remained in the vicinity of the Zapata Swamp. It is known that the Cuban Macaw was persecuted by the native inhabitants. Many birds were shot for food; others were taken from nest holes as nestlings and kept as cage birds. But hunting and nest robbing by the natives cannot be the only reason leading to the extinction of the species in so short a time. A more significant cause of the disappearance of the Cuban Macaw was the intensive plantation farming. Since the eighteenth century, all the accessible lowland areas were used for the production of sugar cane. One must suppose that the Cuban Macaw, which probably was purely a lowland dweller, became confined to the remaining habitat or withdrew to it. The Zapata Swamp, which could not be turned to agricultural purposes, served the birds as a final refuge. Since other cavity-nesting bird species were

also driven out of their original range by the cultivation of sugar cane, one can assume that in the case of the birds of the Zapata Swamp only those bird species capable of adapting have a chance of survival. In the final stages, the Cuban Amazons (*Amazona leucocephala*), which still occurred in great numbers at that time, probably hastened the disappearance of the Cuban Macaw, because the nesting trees in the Zapata Swamp available to both species were occupied mainly by the amazons. It cannot be established to what extent other factors contributed to the decline of the species. It is believed that the last Cuban Macaw died about 1885.

The life history of the Cuban Macaw likely corresponded to those of the related Middle and South American forms. Thus the birds probably wandered about in pairs or in small family units and fed on fruits, seeds, and parts of plants.

Specimens of the Cuban Macaw may be found in

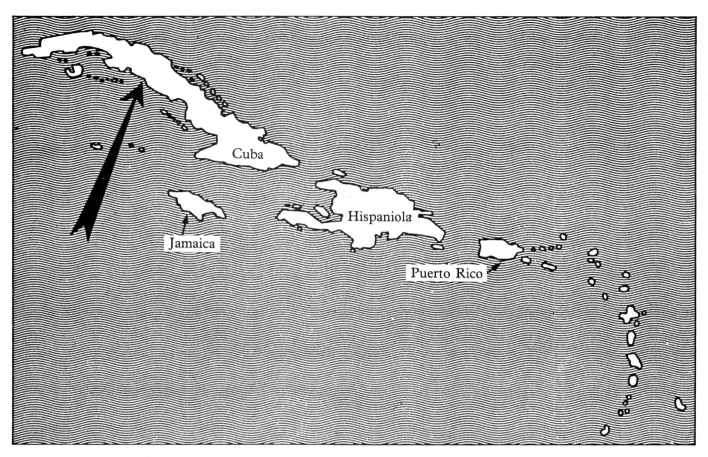

Cuban Macaw *(Ara tricolor)*

the museums of Frankfurt am Main, Dresden, Berlin (GDR), Leyden, Liverpool, London, Vienna, Paris, Stockholm, Cambridge (Massachusetts), New York, Washington, and Havana.

The first report of this macaw is *le petit ara* of d'Aubenton (1779). In Levaillant (1801) it is called *L'ara tricolor*. *Sittace lichtensteini* Wagler 1856 is a synonym. *Ara gossei*, which possibly occurred on Jamaica at that time, could have been a subspecies of *Ara tricolor* (see *Ara gossei*).

Blue-throated Macaw
Ara glaucogularis
Dabbene 1921

Characteristics. Size, about 75 cm. Upper parts from the forehead down to tip of the tail blue. Forehead and forecrown flecked with greenish blue.

Naked reddish cheek and eye region traversed with several lines of greenish blue feathers. From the lower ear region to the throat (bib) bluish green. Narrow yellow orange band from the ear region to the shoulder, merging with the orange yellow underparts. Wings blue, on the underside orange yellow. Under tail coverts blue. Underside of tail feathers orange yellow. Iris yellowish white. Beak black gray. Toes brown black. Female probably like the male, possibly with the throat more bluish. Young birds like adults, but iris brownish; somewhat more slender in body.

Range. Southeastern Beni and western Santa Cruz in Bolivia. Doubtful occurrence in southeastern Tarija (Bolivia), northern Salta, western Formosa, and northwestern Chaco (Argentina).

Remarks. Johann Ingels, Kenneth C. Parkes, and John Farrand, Jr. (1981) conducted detailed research

71

on the "Caninde" Macaw, the separate status of which was in doubt for many years. After evaluating all existing findings and reports, it was established that the macaw described by Wagler in 1832 as *Sittace caninde* (which was already called *Canindé* in 1805 by Azara) could not be the "Caninde" Macaw.

The name *Sittace caninde* Wagler 1832 in the last century principally referred to the Blue-and-yellow Macaws (*Ara ararauna*) from the southernmost part of the range. Dabbene, an Argentinian ornithologist, was the first to point out the contradictions in Azara's remarks. At the same time, W. Bertoni, who thoroughly investigated the supposed locality of the "Caninde" Macaw, northern Paraguay, reported that he encountered only *Ara ararauna*. According to the report of Bertoni, Azara could never have seen the second form ("Caninde" Macaw) of the Blue-and-yellow Macaw. Besides, in the vernacular of the Brazilian populace, the name *caninde* denotes *Ara ararauna*. Dr. Koenig of the Rosenstein Museum in Stuttgart confirms this statement. Ch. Cordier notes that the Guarani Indians refer to the Hyacinth Macaw (*Anodorhynchus hyacinthinus*) as *canindé*.

All the research brought forward by Dabbene clearly indicates that *Sittace caninde* proposed by Wagler is a synonym for *Ara ararauna* (Linnaeus 1758). In 1921, Dabbene unequivocally named the other blue-and-yellow macaw, characterizing it as *glaucogularis*, for both the throat and the upper parts have the same blue green color. Since Dabbene had not designated any type-specimen (which is one of the requirements for ensuring the accuracy of zoological nomenclature), one of the specimens which Dabbene had studied was later so designated. This is Specimen 296 in the Argentine Museum of Natural History in Buenos Aires, which was collected by S. Martin in Santa Cruz de la Sierra in the department of Santa Cruz (Bolivia). This locality also serves as the type-locality of *Ara glaucogularis*. The details furnished by Ingels *et al.* prove that for decades the "Caninde" Macaw was incorrectly named.

The exact range of the Blue-throated Macaw is still not completely known; this probably stems from the long use of the incorrect name and confusion with *Ara ararauna*. Thus, one may be inclined to doubt earlier reports, such as, for example, that of Lynch Arribálzaga (1920), who indicated that this macaw occurred in the area of Rio Bermejo, which separates the Argentine provinces of Formosa and Chaco. Other ornithologists and authors give the range as Misiones (extreme northeastern Argentina) and Paraguay, or even Tarija in southern Bolivia. C. C. Olrog (1979) mentions an occurrence in the Bolivian-Argentine border region, near the city of Yacuiba. G. Hoy (1969) recorded three macaw pairs in a valley of the Rio Carapari in northern Salta, near the Bolivian border; however, he cannot say definitely whether they were *Ara ararauna* or *Ara glaucogularis*. From May to August of 1977, R. S. Ridgely (1980) searched through Bolivia, Argentina, and Paraguay but could not confirm the statements of Hoy and Olrog, as he encountered no macaws in these areas. Ridgely calls the regions of Chuquisaca and Tarija in Bolivia possible localities, and at the same time he cites as an actual locality of the Blue-throated Macaw the environs of the city of Trinidad, or southeast of the city along the Rio Mamoré.

The museum specimens of *Ara glaucogularis*, except those which were labeled with a locality later, all originate from the region cited by Ridgely. Dabbene's specimen comes from Santa Cruz: lat. 17°45′ S, long. 63°14′ W. Both of the specimens collected by J. Steinbach (in the Carnegie Museum of Natural History, Pittsburgh) come from the same region: lat. 17°28′ S, long. 63°37′ W. All the Blue-throated Macaws exported to Central Europe and the United States are said to come from the area of the upper Rio Mamoré in the vicinity of the city of Trinidad, in the department of Beni, Bolivia.

There is no need for further discussion of the distinctness of the Blue-throated Macaw, which was in doubt for years. The author recently had an opportunity to observe about ten Blue-throated Macaws in various enclosures and can therefore make the statement that they are noticeably smaller than the Blue-and-yellow Macaw and that they are far more slender in body as well as in head and beak. The feather pattern on the lore-cheek-eye region is also laid out differently. Four lines of feathers begin below the nostrils and extend over the upper cheek area to the ear; these are very close together. In the Blue-and-yellow Macaw there are only three lines of feathers running vertically in the

Blue-throated Macaw
(Ara glaucogularis)

Bolivia

loral region, very close together. Between the nostrils, the feathers of the forehead extend to the base of the beak; in the Blue-and-yellow Macaw this area is unfeathered for a width of several millimeters. The lower cheek area, which begins at the base of the lower mandible, is bare in the Blue-and-yellow Macaw, but in the Blue-throated Macaw it is completely covered with blue green feathers.

It is also worth mentioning that in almost all birds seen by the author the bare skin area ranged from flesh color to reddish. In the Blue-and-yellow Macaw, these skin parts become red only during excitement or happiness; otherwise these areas are white. The pink tinge of the bare cheeks of Blue-throated Macaws may be characteristic of young birds. Unfortunately, as of this writing, no data on the breeding behavior of the Blue-throated Macaw or its habits have been recorded, so no comparison can be made with the Blue-and-yellow Macaw. Further proof of the separate status of the Blue-throated Macaw is that throughout its range, or at least in part of it, the species forms small mixed flocks with the Blue-and-yellow Macaw and possibly even with the Scarlet Macaw (*Ara macao*).

Way of Life. For several decades there were many mysteries about the Blue-throated Macaw. As little was known about its distribution as about its status as a distinct species. As research undertaken a short time ago shows, for years, the Blue-and-yellow Macaw was, in the southern part of its range, confused with the Blue-throated Macaw, and thus the range of the latter was given as Paraguay, southern Bolivia, and extreme northwestern Argentina. As previously mentioned, this error has finally been cleared up. As currently known, the range of the Blue-throated Macaw extends for a narrow stretch from southeastern Beni, southeast of the city of Trinidad (capital of the department of Beni) in a southeasterly direction along the Rio Mamoré and its tributaries, toward central-western Santa Cruz, north of the cities of Santa Cruz and Buena Vista. The range of the Blue-throated Macaw is limited by the *yungas*, the cloud forests at the foothills of the Eastern Cordilleras. One could describe the landscape as *llanos*. This warm lowland dotted with swamps—open woodland which gives way toward the south to "forest islands" (*montes*) and gallery forests which are interspersed with grass

savannas—is the natural habitat of the Blue-throated Macaw. The Blue-throated Macaw lives in this area along with the Blue-and-yellow Macaw (*Ara ararauna*) and the Scarlet Macaw (*Ara macao*). It is evident that the Blue-throated Macaw occupies the same ecological niche as the two other macaw species, which leads to the conclusion that in this favorable habitat an abundant supply of food is at their disposal. The Blue-throated Macaw is a rare species in its range of about 3000 km², and thus one supposes that the Blue-and-yellow Macaw is a hundred times more plentiful than the Blue-throated Macaw. Citing Romero, Ridgely notes that it often forms mixed flocks with the Blue-and-yellow. The life cycle of this extremely rare macaw probably corresponds to that of related species. The breeding season probably begins in December and lasts until the young birds leave the nest in April. It's conceivable that the range of the Blue-throated Macaw continues across Santa Cruz southward through southwestern Chuquisaca and eastern Tarija in southeastern Bolivia, possibly to northern Salta, northwestern Formosa, and extreme northwestern Chaco in Argentina, and possibly into the Bolivian-Paraguayan border area in extreme southeastern Bolivia. At any rate, there are no reports of Blue-throated Macaws from this last area in recent times, and it is not clear whether the statements made in earlier years were about *Ara glaucogularis* or *Ara ararauna*.

Care and Breeding. Blue-throated Macaws were considered "mythical" birds until a short time ago. Only scattered skins in a few natural-history museums (among others, in the British Museum of Natural History, Tring) bore witness to the existence of these birds. The bird park at Walsrode was the first zoological garden to be successful in obtaining Blue-throated Macaws and to exhibit them in the parrot house. Thereafter, some light could be shed on the darkness that surrounded this parrot species. It soon became clear that we were not dealing with young of the Blue-and-yellow Macaw, although it was initially supposed that the Blue-throated Macaw might possibly represent the juvenile of a subspecies of the Blue-and-yellow Macaw. In 1979 and 1980, some of these macaws could still be imported, at a price hovering somewhere around DM 10,000 each. The estimated population of these macaws in the Federal Republic of Germany is fifteen to twenty birds. These are in the hands of private breeders as well as in the bird park at Walsrode and the Berlin Zoo.

The Blue-throated Macaw is a very active bird, far more agile than other large macaw species. In the spring of 1981, the author was able to observe a group of four of these macaws in the bird park at Walsrode. Three of the birds got along very well with each other, but the fourth macaw kept apart — perhaps it was not tolerated by the other three — and continuously plucked its shoulder feathers. Since the bird clung to the mesh front of the aviary all the time, it could be observed most carefully. Nothing would stop its plucking activity. It gnawed at its feathers almost pathologically and injured the skin beneath. The cause of this abnormal behavior could not be discerned. Perhaps a fungus disease produced extreme skin irritation, or maybe a purely psychological disorder caused the bird to gnaw at its feathers and skin.

It is to be hoped that the few fanciers possessing these rare macaws will soon be successful in their breeding attempts with these animals, so that the experiences already accumulated can be enriched and enlarged.

Blue-and-yellow Macaw
Ara ararauna
(Linnaeus 1758)

Characteristics. Size, about 90 cm. Upper parts blue. Lower parts yellow. Forehead and forecrown green, changing into blue. The bare eye and cheek region extends from the base of the upper and lower mandibles to the ear region. In the upper part of the bare area three black lines of feathers extend from the base of the upper mandible to the ear region. In the loral region several lines of feathers run vertically to the forehead. The lower cheek region is completely bare. From the ear region to the throat, a band olive green to black. Ear region, sides of neck, breast, and belly yellow to orange yellow. Occiput, nape, back, wings, rump, under tail coverts and upper side of tail blue. Underside of wings olive yellow. Iris yellow. Bare facial areas white. Beak black. Toes gray black. Female somewhat more slender; head and beak flatter; forehead tinged with green brown (not confirmed as a sex-specific characteristic). Young birds like adults; smaller; brown iris.

Range. Eastern Panama. Colombia west and east of the Andes. Southward along the Andes to southeastern Bolivia. Eastward from Venezuela, south of the Orinoco, to Trinidad, Guyana, Suriname, French Guiana, and Brazil. Southward to northern Paraguay. Possibly northern Chaco (Argentina) and southeastern Bolivia.

Remarks. Until a short time ago it was unclear whether the Blue-and-yellow Macaws in the southwestern part of the range constituted a subspecies, the "Caninde" Macaw. Results of the latest research demonstrate unequivocally the separate status of both species (see *Ara glaucogularis*). Still, perhaps there are races of the Blue-and-yellow Macaw in its very extensive flatland range. It has struck the author that the birds from the northwestern part of South America, with their bright orange yellow breast feathers, differ markedly from those of the more southerly areas, which are more yellowish in color. Furthermore, the birds of the northwest are larger and have a heavier build.

Way of Life. The Blue-and-yellow Macaw, conspicuous throughout its range because of its coloration, is often found only locally. In recent years more and more of these birds are being driven out of their original range, and thus they have been extirpated from many areas where they formerly were common.

In Panama, east of the Canal Zone, Blue-and-yellow Macaws are found in the river valleys of the Cordillera de San Blas, the Serrania del Darién, and the Serrania del Sapo. This area, which only rises to about 1000 m., offers a very wide variety of biotopes. The Blue-and-yellow Macaws live here in mangrove swamps, virgin forests, and savannas, which only very rarely are broken up by plantations. In Colombia, the Blue-and-yellow Macaws are encountered mainly in the delta of the Atrato at the Gulf of the Urabá and further south in the river valleys of the western Andean slopes. On the Pacific side it is found as far as the department of Narino, which borders Ecuador. In

Blue-and-yellow Macaw
(Ara ararauna)

northeastern Colombia these macaws favor the valleys in which the Magdalena originates. The Sierra de Perijá and the Sierra Nevada de Santa Marta form a natural boundary of the range in northwestern Venezuela. In eastern and southeastern Colombia one finds the macaws in lowlands of the Orinoco and Amazon tributaries east of the Andes. In a southerly direction the range continues east of the Andes to southern Bolivia, possibly even to the province of Chaco in Argentina. From the regions of eastern Colombia, eastern Peru, and eastern Bolivia there are very few reports of the occurrence of Blue-and-yellow Macaws. Obviously, in these vast, inaccessible regions, observing the birds in the wild is an extremely adventurous undertaking; however, despite this handicap one must make the supposition that Blue-and-yellow Macaws are not so common in the regions just mentioned as in northern Colombia or Guyana.

In southeastern Beni and western Santa Cruz (Bolivia), the Blue-and-yellow Macaw lives in the same areas as the Scarlet Macaw (*Ara macao*) and the Blue-throated Macaw (*Ara glaucogularis*) and here forms small parties with these other species. In this locality, as in most of the range of the Blue-and-yellow Macaw, there are groves of buriti palms (*Mauritia* sp.), from which ripe and semiripe fruits serve as the dietary staple of the macaws. In the Beni area, hybrids of Blue-and-yellow and Scarlet macaws often occur.

In Paraguay, Blue-and-yellow Macaws reach the central lowlands between the Paraná and the Paraguay, the southernmost part of their vast range. The Neembucú Swamp area is still fully intact, since human settlement or agricultural ventures would be hopeless in this area. Other areas which are still intact and inhabited by the animals are found north of the capital of Asunción and the adjacent chaco to the west. Some ornithologists assume that the Blue-and-yellow Macaw has already been extirpated from Paraguay.

The species occurs throughout Brazil, with the exception of the states of Rio Grand de Norte, Paraíba, eastern Pernambuco, Algoas, and Sergipe, as well as along the Atlantic coastal strip to the south. In Brazil, as in the other parts of its range, Blue-and-yellow Macaws principally inhabit wooded riverine areas, avoiding large tracts of unbroken

forest. The Blue-and-yellow Macaws are the most numerous member of their genus in uncolonized regions of central Goiás and southern Mato Grosso. In the opinion of Pinto and Camargo (1948) they are the only macaw species found in large areas of Mato Grosso.

Over a long period of time, P. Roth examined in detail the feeding habits of native parrots in the Rio Aripuanã region. The Blue-and-yellow Macaw he sees as a dietary generalist that shows tendencies toward specialization.

The Blue-and-yellow Macaw (*Ara ararauna*) gets the main bulk of its nourishment from the fruits of various palm species. Most important of all are the inajá palms (*Maximiliana regia*) and the tucumã palms (*Astrocaryum* sp.). Of the latter, the oily liquid in the kernels of the unripened fruit and also the flesh of fully ripened fruit are eaten. The buriti palm (*Mauritia* sp.) may play an important role, because I frequently observed an *Ara ararauna* pair in the same buriti palm that was "headquarters" for *Ara manilata*. However, I could never confirm my supposition by direct observation of them feeding.

During the dry season, the Blue-and-yellow Macaws fulfill their need for minerals—sodium in particular —on the steep banks of the Rio Branco, at so-called *barreiros*, where the mineral-rich earth is at the surface.

In French Guiana, Suriname, and Guyana, the Blue-and-yellow Macaws live in coastal regions covered with mangrove swamps as well as in the wooded river valleys of the interior. In Venezuela these macaws are limited to the region south of the Orinoco, as well as the Orinoco Delta.

In Trinidad, Blue-and-yellow Macaws occur in extremely small numbers. Prior to 1959, ffrench (1976) reports, small flocks of up to fifteen birds could often be observed; after that the population declined drastically. It is feared that in the near future Blue-and-yellow Macaws will be extirpated from Trinidad. There are still a few macaws on the island, which are completely under the protection of the government; the question is, however, who will oversee the enforcement of such a law in this country. Many times in past years the author visited Trinidad but could not observe any macaws in the Nariva Swamp, a small mangrove swamp area in the eastern part of the island which is the final refuge of the macaws. Probably eighty percent of the deplorable decline of the macaws on Trinidad can be traced to nest robbing. It is very easy to locate the animals, as they always make their loud calls during flight; it is also a simple matter to discover breeding sites and to take the young birds from the nests. The author was able to see Blue-and-yellow Macaws in the possession of many native animal fanciers and at one animal dealer's. The dealer admitted that nowadays he can no longer obtain macaws from Trinidad; the Blue-and-yellow Macaws that he sometimes sells are always brought to him by fishermen who go trapping along the coasts of Venezuela and Guyana. It should be recognized that in Trinidad the Blue-and yellow Macaw is given no chance of survival. Even if one assumes that at least two or three breeding pairs are still present, which is probably doubtful, these pairs will lose most of their offspring annually due to nest robbing or environmental factors; that the species will thus die out is preordained and not preventable.

On the island of Tobago, which lies northeast of Trinidad, a bird fancier keeps several Blue-and-yellow Macaws at liberty (on Tobago there are no indigenous Blue-and-yellow Macaws). These birds are almost completely self-sufficient, but they are provided with a supplement of some seeds and nuts, which are available in the owner's garden. The birds are kept completely free, and they often stray from their part of the small island. The author was able to observe the macaws in flight, and he can understand perfectly why Haverschmidt (1954) describes the flight of Blue-and-yellow Macaws as particularly impressive. They always present a remarkable spectacle to the eye of the beholder, with slow-beating wings raised no higher than their bodies, long trailing tails, and blue and orange feathers gleaming in the sunlight. All the macaws kept on Tobago and Trinidad displayed very intensely orange breast and belly feathers. The author has never observed such an intensity of color in Blue-and-yellow Macaws in captivity in Europe, even though a large number of the birds kept by us come from the same tropical area, namely, Guyana. It is conceivable that the constant high humidity, combined with high temperatures night and day, permits the color to develop to the fullest.

On the South American continent the Blue-and-yellow Macaw is not threatened to the same degree that it is, for example, on Trinidad, but a decline in numbers is reported from all parts of its range. The fundamental reason for this, as for other animal and plant species, is the permanent alteration (destruction) of the environment. An additional factor which adds to the threat to the Blue-and-yellow Macaw population is the fact that, due to their "sociable" nature, they are popular as cage or aviary birds—and not only in North America and Europe. In South America they are thought to be just as desirable. In the opinion of the author, South America is where the greatest number of large parrots are kept in captivity. The "demand" for house pets has to have an effect on the population living in the wild. If the living space is still intact, occasional capture of animals for fanciers on the whole does not threaten the general population. The chief danger, as always, is the despoiling of nature through environmental changes.

The Blue-and-yellow Macaws are gregarious birds that during the day move around in small flocks or in pairs, foraging. In late afternoon they will fly to roosting trees where they spend the night. Often more than a hundred macaws may gather in such locations, and their loud cries can be heard for great distances.

The breeding season of the Blue-and-yellow Macaws occurs at different times in the various parts of their extensive range. In the northernmost regions, such as Panama, Trinidad, Guyana, etc., breeding may begin in February, although often not until March. In southern parts of their range, mating can be observed in December or January. In northern Paraguay, one of the southernmost parts, the macaws begin to seek a nest site about the end of October or the beginning of November. Egg laying takes place in mid-November. As a rule, two to four eggs are laid, usually in tree cavities, and are incubated for about twenty-seven days by the hen. The cock does not participate in incubation. Eggs are laid at intervals of two or three days; the hen usually begins incubation after laying the second egg. Rearing the young takes eighty to ninety days, with both parents taking part in feeding. Upon leaving the nest, the young are fully capable of flight, and during the first days they are distinguishable from their parents only by their somewhat shorter tails. The parents still feed and take care of the offspring for several more weeks. A short time after leaving the nest, the young are introduced into the macaw flock. During the first few weeks parents and young stay very close together, and one can notice that they mostly sit close to one another and fly together.

P. Roth, who lived for quite a long period in one part of the range of *Ara ararauna*—the Rio Aripauanã in northern Mato Grosso—recording the behavioral patterns of the parrots living there, informed the author that he had received a young bird which was between seventy and eighty days old in mid-November from Índios. Roth believes that the breeding season of the Blue-and-yellow Macaws in western Mato Grosso begins in July or August and ends sometime around the end of the year.

Care and Breeding. The Blue-and-yellow Macaw is one of the most popular cage birds. Next to the Grey Parrot (*Psittacus erithacus*) and some amazon species (*Amazona*), it is one of the most widely kept large parrots. Because of its pleasing coloration, relatively good talking ability, and, most of all, of its "lovable disposition," the Blue-and-yellow Macaw has many devotees. The majority of the birds offered in the trade are young and already tame. Since singly kept birds lack a mate, they attach themselves to the person who owns them and see in him a substitute. Since Blue-and-yellow Macaws are very gregarious, it is vital that the owner be around the bird as much as possible. As soon as a macaw is left alone, it screams for its mate, the owner. With the advent of sexual maturity, the Blue-and-yellow Macaw shows an especially strong attachment to one person, a behavior more clearly evident in male animals than in females. Blue-and-yellow Macaws are very playful birds and can occupy themselves with an object for hours. If a Blue-and-yellow Macaw is allowed an "excursion" in the garden, one can observe how the macaw waddles across the lawn and then in some place, mainly near a tree trunk, suddenly uses its beak to dig a hole in the earth and thus keeps busy for a long time. The author has observed Blue-and-yellow Macaws making friends with dogs and playing with them for hours.

Blue-and-yellow Macaws are one of the few macaw species that are relatively easy to breed. As

early as 1921, Karl Neunzig reported successful Blue-and-yellow Macaw breedings. In Caen, France, between 1818 and 1822, a Blue-and-yellow Macaw produced twenty-five chicks in the course of nineteen (!) breedings. The female laid up to six eggs each time, and thus in the space of three-and-a-half years, sixty-two eggs were laid. In view of the fact that the birds were kept only in a cage, this success seems all the more remarkable. Neunzig estimates the incubation period of Blue-and-yellow Macaws to be twenty to twenty-five days. Nowadays we know that the incubation normally takes twenty-five to thirty days. The nestling period of the "French" macaws lasted about ninety days, which accords with our present knowledge.

Successful breedings occur regularly in European countries and in North America, where they are mostly achieved in zoological gardens. Especially in animal parks, hybrids are bred, because here macaws of various species are housed together. The zoological garden of the city of Wuppertal achieved a notable success in this respect. A breeding pair consisting of a Blue-and-yellow Macaw and a Red-and-green Macaw have reared forty young birds between 1963 and 1980 (in the section on the Red-and-green Macaw (*Ara chloroptera*), these hybrid offspring will be treated in greater detail).

In 1978, H. Linn had the pleasure of the first pure breeding of the Blue-and-yellow Macaw in Germany. When two hand-tame Blue-and-yellow Macaws were placed in an aviary together, they began to court one another. Both birds became aggressive toward the owner and responded to his presence by snapping at him with their beaks. Since both macaws also showed themselves to be quite aggressive toward other birds in the aviary, they were transferred to new quarters and given a nest box (45 x 45 x 110 cm.). The nest box evoked the greatest interest from both animals; immediately after installation they examined it in the minutest detail. On February 1, about a month after the installation of the nest box, the first egg (36.0 x 50.0 mm.) was laid. The second and third eggs were laid at intervals of three days. Since the aviary lacked heat and outdoor temperatures stayed at −15 C., breeding was not successful. Inspection of the clutch showed three infertile eggs; these were removed thirty days after the beginning of incubation. Beginning March 16, three new eggs were laid at the same intervals as before. Again, copulation had not been observed, but on the eighteenth day, inspection showed that all of the eggs had been fertilized. The first chick hatched after an incubation period of thirty days, while the second chick emerged six days later. One embryo died. Incubation was tight from the first day of egg laying, and it lasted exactly thirty days; thus it was the second egg that did not hatch.

The young birds were completely naked. The upper mandible was light and projected into an equally light, shovel-shaped, lower mandible. The beak did not start to become colored until the birds were fifteen days old. By the age of twenty-five days, the first feather sheaths emerged. Both birds were weighed at eight and nine weeks of age, and the scale registered 1075 and 1125 grams respectively. During this time feathering also made very rapid progress. The appetite of the young birds seemed boundless, and the amount of food fed to them increased tenfold. Egg food mixed with dog kibble (Bio-Hundeflocken) was added to the customary seed, fruit, berries, and zwieback. Rearing followed a smooth course, and the offspring left the nest at the age of ninety days. Although the young birds were capable of eating independently, they were still fed by the adults. Three weeks after fledging, the breeding cock attacked one of the young birds, and in the following days its aggressiveness towards this youngster increased. To prevent injury, the young bird had to be separated. Presumably it was a male which the breeding cock saw as a rival.

In 1972, one chick was successfully reared in Switzerland (Kirchhofer 1973). An indoor flight 3 m³ and an outdoor flight 7.0 x 4.0 x 3.5 m. high housed the two Blue-and-yellow Macaws. These birds reacted to every impending change of weather with loud screeches. Although there was hope that these two birds would become a pair and produce young, one shuddered to think what their increased screaming during breeding would be like and whether this would finally shatter the patience of the neighbors. An 80-liter wine barrel with an entrance hole of 15 cm., set up about two meters high, greatly interested the birds. Copulation was seen only occasionally. Both birds would hang by one foot on the aviary mesh, use the other foot to grasp each other, and then rub their lower bellies together. The author also has observed other large macaw species copulating in this fashion. During copulation an impressive play with the eyes takes place. The pupils are narrowed to the size of pinpoints, and the mate nimbly extends its wings and thrusts its beak out. Each time this is done, one can hear a satisfied *ooh*.

The first eggs laid by the "Swiss" Blue-and-yellow Macaws were infertile. Both eggs, which weighed approximately 28 g., were removed. The second laying was a success, with one young chick growing up and developing splendidly. During the incubation and nestling periods the parent birds kept very quiet, to avoid attracting the attention of enemies to themselves or to their offspring. In the wild this behavior affords animals the greatest possible chance of survival.

Parent birds do not always rear their young. Young pairs especially, breeding for the first time, are quite clumsy in their behavior. Blue-and-yellow Macaws become sexually mature at about six years of age; i.e., Blue-and-yellow Macaw hens that have grown up in captivity lay their first eggs in their sixth year. The author, however, has observed courtship behavior in much younger birds. It is almost a rule that the first clutch laid is infertile. Similarly, there are usually complications the first time young are reared: the chicks are not fed enough; or the female stays outside the nest box too often, so that the young are not kept warm enough; or the youngsters may be crushed or injured by the still somewhat clumsy behavior of the young parents.

The English breeder J. M. Edgar described (in *Cage and Aviary Birds*) the successful hand-rearing of a Blue-and-yellow Macaw from the first day of life, which demanded an incredible amount of time and patience. Until the eighteenth day of life, the chick was fed every two hours. Since the little bird stayed in an artificial nest and also got soiled in the course of feedings, it had to be cleaned each time it was fed. From the nineteenth to the twenty-fifth day of the chick's life, feeding took place every three hours; after that, the chick was fed at four-hour intervals. Edgar recorded the development of the chick chronologically. On the second day of life the chick weighed 17 g.; on the fifth, 30 g.; on the seventh, 50 g.; on the eleventh, 70 g. At the age of two weeks it was already 85 g.; at three weeks, 220

The Blue-and-yellow Macaw *(Ara ararauna)* is famed for having a lovable disposition. Five-year-old Jeffrey Frohock helped to train Tequilla.

g.; and at the age of eight weeks, it tipped the scales at 380 g. Blue-and-yellow Macaws can attain a weight of 1300 g. Young birds leaving the nest at ninety days generally weigh from 800 to 1000 g.

One of the most successful German macaw breeders (forty-nine Illiger's Macaws by the end of 1981), Herr Veser of Tettnang, also succeeded in 1981 in breeding the Blue-and-yellow Macaw. In 1976, he obtained a pair approximately seven years old from Colombia. The birds were housed in a double-wired indoor flight which measured 2.6 x 1.2 x 2.0–2.5 m. high, with a 4.0 x 1.2 x 1.8 m. high outdoor flight. The cock could be distinguished from the hen only his broader, longer, and sturdier tail and her lesser weight. The female weighed 1.0 kg.; the cock, 1.2 kg.

For three years every means was employed to create optimal conditions for the macaws to breed. In 1978, the birds moved into the nest box installed in the indoor flight. In March, eggs were laid. Result: the eggs were fertile, got damaged, and died. In 1979, egg laying again took place in March, with the temperature at 20 C. inside. In order to raise the humidity, the nest box was repeatedly sprayed with water. This clutch was also unsuccessful. In 1980, the hen again laid her eggs in March. The nest log was kept moist, and, in addition, the indoor flight was sprayed regularly. Again the effort resulted in failure.

In 1980–81, the birds overwintered without heat. The nest box, now situated in the outdoor flight, was 45 cm. in diameter and 70 cm. high inside, with a 16 cm. entrance hole. It was set into the ground and provided with a timed sprinkler apparatus that came on for short periods at 1 p.m. and 4 p.m. In order to delay egg laying, less vitamin E was given in the spring. Egg laying occurred in June. The hitherto tame Blue-and-yellow Macaws now became aggressive and prone to biting. It took deception and trickery to enter the aviary to take care of feeding and nest-box inspections. During disturbances the cock always stationed himself in front of the hen, in order to frighten and ward off supposed enemies. Copulation could be observed several times daily, with the birds sitting next to each other, holding each other with the left and right feet and rubbing their vents together; however, only one egg, 49 x 40 mm., was fertile. During the incubation period, the cock always sat close to the nest box and kept watch. Any disturbance provoked a murderous outcry, followed by the hen emerging from the nest box to support the cock with powerful screeching. If the flight was entered, both animals would retreat to the nest box to defend the eggs.

After an incubation period of twenty-seven days, a chick emerged on July 19, weighing 30 g. Even on the first day it had a few white down feathers on its lower back and a few on its head. After fourteen days, the chick weighed 69 g. By this time all of the down was shed, and the feather sheaths had broken through the skin. During the chick's first week, the cock fed only the hen, but later he also fed the chick. The young bird feathered in rapidly after the twentieth day, with the wing and tail feathers and feathers on the head growing more rapidly than the others. At fifty-five days, the tail feathers were about 10 cm. long, and the chick weighed 1100 g. On October 12, just three months after its birth, weighing 1000 g., the chick flew out of the nest. After it had left the nest, the youngster was still fed by the parents for three more months, even though it was self-sufficient.

The Bleil family has owned a completely normally colored breeding pair of Blue-and-yellow Macaws for a long time. When these animals first bred, two eggs were laid. Both eggs hatched, and both chicks were reared by the parents without difficulty. One chick from the brood exhibited normal coloration; but in the case of the second chick, all feathers that would have normally been blue were brown black. This situation was repeated with the second breeding. The third breeding resulted in only one chick reaching maturity; this bird, like the two chicks from the first and second broods, was colored brown black. This "degeneration" in feather color can be traced back to melanism. Melanism can also show up in people, producing a dark color in the skin or mucous membranes through the deposition of melanin or similar pigments. This can occur in cases of Basedow's disease, pregnancy, etc. In birds the brown black feather color is the result of one pigment. This form of melanism is known chiefly in the Papuan Lory (*Charmosyna papou goliathina*), from the highlands of central New Guinea, in which all red-feathered parts are brown black instead. Abnormal feather appearance can also be observed in St. Vincent Amazons (*Amazona guildingii*) living in the wild on St. Vincent in the West Indies.

The zoological garden of Baranquilla, Colombia, has a Blue-and-yellow Macaw that has white breast feathers. The zoo also owns a Yellow-crowned Amazon (*Amazona ochrocephala panamensis*) in which the usually green feathers are completely blue.

Hybrid breedings have occurred very often. Zoos time and again report successful hybrid breedings with the Red-and-green Macaw (*Ara chloroptera*) and the Scarlet Macaw (*Ara macao*), but less frequently with the Great Green Macaw (*Ara ambigua*) and the Military Macaw (*A. militaris*).

Red-fronted Macaw
Ara rubrogenys
Lafresnaye 1847

Characteristics. Size, about 60 cm. Olive green. Head and nape more yellow olive green. Forehead to crown dark red. Ear patch dark red. Unfeathered facial area very restricted, with only narrow bare streaks between the base of the beak and the eye. Bare skin area marked with lines of dark feathers. Carpal edge, bend of wing, and shoulder coverts orange red. Primaries and outer secondaries blue on the outer vanes. Inner vanes of primaries becoming black. Underside of wings olive green. Breast and belly often flecked with red feathers. Thighs orange red. Tail feathers olive green, blue toward the tip, dark olive green on the underside at the base, becoming black. Iris orange. Bare skin area around the eyes white. Beak black. Toes black brown. Female possibly somewhat more slender; the red on the forehead and crown possibly not as intense; bare skin area between the beak and the eyes possibly not so finely marked with lines of dark feathers. Young birds probably like adults.

Range. Bolivia: southeastern Cochabamba and possibly southwestern Santa Cruz.

Way of Life. To judge from old reports, which are extremely few, the rare Red-fronted Macaws would seem to live in the cloud forests of Las Yungas in the fertile high valleys of the eastern Andes in the department of Cochabamba in central Bolivia. Instead, the habitat of the Red-fronted Macaw has a different character: it encompasses the dry valleys of the southern Eastern Cordilleras in the southeastern part of the department of Cochabamba and may also extend to southwestern Santa Cruz. In this area, in which this rare species lives at altitudes between 1300 and 2200 m., predominatedly dry forests and scrub with cacti are encountered. Only during the rainy season do the usually dry rivers and streams send much rainwater in the direction of the Gran Chaco.

In the canyonlike valleys of the "broken *puna*," the Red-fronted Macaws outside the breeding season live in flocks of up to eighty animals, as they wander nomadically through their small range, foraging for food. Ridgely estimates this area at 50 x 100 km. Fruit from trees, bushes, and some cacti constitute the main part of their diet. Red-fronted Macaws also come to the ground for some of their food; in this they differ markedly from other species of the genus, which chiefly feed on the fruits of trees and palms. In some of the small settled areas in the biotope of the Red-fronted Macaw, peanuts and corn are cultivated. The macaws invade these fields when the fruits ripen. With their beaks they dig out the peanuts growing underground, causing significant damage and thus becoming unwanted "guests." The Indian populace living in this region, therefore, set traps for the macaws. They go after these animals not only because of the damage they do to crops but also for their meat and their feathers.

The breeding season of the Red-fronted Macaws begins with the onset of the rainy season in October. Cavities in the steep, canyonlike mountain slopes are their principal nest sites. There is no information about their nesting habits. But in recent years professional trappers have caught a great number of adult and young birds, or caused them to be caught, and thus could obtain some insight into the birds' way of life. Unfortunately, such "specialists" remain silent, as profit takes precedence.

Care and Breeding. It was probably Charles Cordier, a scientifically trained animal trapper, who, early in the 1970s sent the first Red-fronted Macaws to Europe. (Cordier had stopped in

Stages of growth of a Blue-and-yellow Macaw *(Ara ararauna)*, with its happy breeder, F. Veser.

1, 2. The wild population of Red-fronted Macaws *(Ara rubrogenys)* is estimated to be 3000 animals at most. Large numbers of these parrots were captured for export in recent years, and it may be feared that this species will become extinct. An absolute ban on trapping and hunting offers the only chance for the survival of the Red-fronted Macaw.

Red-fronted Macaw
(Ara rubrogenys)

Bolivia

Cochabamba, Bolivia, in order to collect the Andean Cock-of-the-Rock, *Rupicola peruviana saturata*.) In 1972, Dr. Burkard of Zurich received a pair of Red-fronted Macaws that Cordier was able to capture. The male had a broken wing and was being cared for in a cage set up outdoors; the female soon visited her mate and so was captured as well. About the same time, or somewhat later, the bird park at Walsrode, the Wuppertaler Zoo, and the zoological garden in Berlin also acquired these rare macaws. In England and the United States, Red-fronted Macaws were exhibited in zoological gardens about this time. A few years later the birds were offered for sale in the animal trade. The price of these macaws is very high, as much as for the Hyacinth Macaw (*Anodorhynchus hyacinthinus*). R. S. Ridgely (1980, citing Nilsson and Mack) reports that in recent years great numbers of these birds have been captured. The United States alone received 16 birds in 1977, 82 in 1978, and 125 in the first eight months of 1979. It is irresponsible to take such a large number of live specimens for export purposes when the wild population is at most 3000 birds.

During acclimation Red-fronted Macaws are very sensitive. The author once obtained a Red-fronted Macaw which was just released from quarantine. It was only with the greatest difficulty that the bird could be acclimated. In the beginning it would eat only sunflower seeds; if it was disturbed while eating, it would immediately vomit these. Only in the course of time, by very gradual stages, did the bird slowly become accustomed to eating other kinds of food. Corn, especially in the half-ripe stage, became its preferred food. It took a very long time until the bird lost its fear. It never became tame and always maintained a large fleeing distance. Rose hips, which, unfortunately, are available for only a short period of time, became its favorite food, but even these were never accepted if offered by hand. The bird was quiet; it was never moved by the screams of the other macaws to join in. When, after a short time, no mate of its species could be found, the bird was turned over to a Swiss parrot fancier who was building up a stock of Red-fronted Macaws. As of this writing (1981) no breeding attempts have yet been made.

The courtship behavior of Red-fronted Macaws is an interesting spectacle. When the wings are held out, the orange red at the bend of the wing assumes full importance. The cock struts back and forth on the branch (perch), emitting shrill whistling sounds. The pupils of the eyes become so sharply narrowed that the bright orange iris stands out. Courting can last ten to fifteen minutes and ends with the hen being fed by the cock, and then copulation follows.

The zoological garden of the city of Wuppertal owns the only known breeding pair of Red-fronted Macaws. In 1978 this pair bred for the first time. Dr. Schürer of the zoo told the author that in 1978 three Red-fronted Macaw chicks were hand-reared by their keepers, Herr and Frau Bock. In 1979, the macaw pair raised two youngsters without any help. In 1980, the macaws again reared two young birds, but, unfortunately, one chick died a short while after it left the nest, because it was not properly fed. In the spring of 1981, the zoo had a total of ten Red-fronted Macaws in its stock, of which six birds had been raised in Wuppertal. The Wilhelma, the zoological garden in Stuttgart, exhibits some of the "Wuppertal" offspring in its new parrot section.

It is encouraging that some German parrot fanciers have been able to accumulate a small stock of Red-fronted Macaws in recent years, so that in the near future successful breeding can be expected.

Chestnut-fronted Macaw
Ara severa
(Linnaeus 1758)

Two subspecies:

1. *Ara severa severa* (Linnaeus)

Characteristics. Size, about 46 cm. Green. Forehead reddish brown. Forecrown bluish green. Brownish line running from chin to ear region borders the bare facial area. Bend of wing, carpal edge, and under wing coverts scarlet red. Outer vanes of primaries and secondaries blue. Outer vanes of the outer greater primary coverts blue. Underside of wings reddish brown. Lower feathers of thighs red. Under tail coverts blue green. Tail feathers red brown, greenish at the base. Underside of tail feathers dark orange red. Bare cheek-eye region yellowish white, traversed with many lines of

The head study of these two Chestnut-fronted Macaws *(Ara severa)* clearly shows the arrangement of the lines of black feathers on the bare facial patch.

1, 6. Blue-throated Macaw *(Ara glaucogularis).* This species has become available to aviculture only recently and in small numbers. 2. Military Macaw *(Ara militaris).* 3. Hyacinth Macaw *(Anodorhynchus hyacinthinus).* 4. Recently imported Yellow-collared Macaws *(Ara auricollis).* 5. Scarlet Macaw with primaries trimmed to prevent flight.

black feathers. Iris brownish red. Beak black gray. Feet gray. Female like the male, but reddish brown front narrower; somewhat more slender. Young birds like adults; the reddish brown forehead, however, is not present in the young female, since the forehead becomes fully colored only in the second or third year; the iris is brownish, then becomes light, and afterwards brownish red.

Range. North central Venezuela eastward to French Guiana. Southward to northwestern Mato Grosso, northern Goiás, and northwestern Bahia (Brazil).

2. *Ara severa castaneifrons* Lafresnaye

Characteristics. Like the nominate subspecies, but larger.

Range. Eastern Panama. Colombia, along the Atrato and the Caribbean coast, as well as east of the Andes southwards to eastern Peru and northern Bolivia. Western Venezuala southward to northwestern Mato Grosso (Brazil).

Way of Life. The Chestnut-fronted Macaw is a bird which is encountered quite often in various localities in its range. An inhabitant of purely tropical-zone landscapes, it prefers the virgin forests along rivers. The course of its day is the same as that of related species. In the morning, small flocks move off in different directions from the sleeping places, usually large freestanding broadleaf trees or palms which have been used for a long time. Groups of five to twenty animals forage through a wide area around the sleeping place.

At the Rio Aripuanã in far northern Mato Grosso, where the ranges of the two geographic races overlap, P. Roth studied the feeding habits of *Ara severa*. Roth reported that the Chestnut-fronted Macaw competes for food with the large macaws present there (*A. ararauna*, *A. chloroptera*, and *A. macao*) and even with the Red-bellied Macaw (*A. manilata*), since its food consists mostly of the fruits of many palms which these other macaws also consume. At the same time, *Ara severa* eats fruits which are also eaten by *Pyrrhura*, *Aratinga*, *Pionus*, and *Amazona* species, etc. The birds enjoy invading

orchards, where they cause considerable damage. Since they are considered agricultural pests, Chestnut-fronted Macaws are ruthlessly hunted with shotguns by farmers. The birds have an advantage in that while eating, resting, or preening, they are very hard to recognize, since all these are done silently. Only during flight do they voice their calls, which probably serve to keep the flock together. Long flights are not undertaken by the macaws during the day, probably because of fear of enemies, such as people or birds of prey. As soon as the birds have settled in the foliage, their green color is very difficult to make out. In the late afternoon hours the return flight back to the roost takes place. Since the sleeping trees are often used by more than a hundred birds, much screeching takes place in the course of altercations for the best sleeping places. Each group coming in later causes another uproar.

In Panama, Chestnut-fronted Macaws live to the east and south of the Canal Zone in the undeveloped, virgin tropical forest areas. The presence of these birds north and west of the Panama Canal can no longer be confirmed (Eisenmann and Loftin 1968), although they had been found there previously. In southwestern Panama, Chestnut-fronted Macaws have been observed together with Blue-headed Parrots (*Pionus menstruus rubrigularis*). In Panama, the breeding season begins in February and March. In northern Colombia, the Chestnut-fronted Macaws begin to breed earlier, in January and February. Abandoned woodpecker holes or the holes in dead palm trees often serve as nesting places.

In Colombia these macaws are more commonly found east of the Andes, in the region of the headwaters of the Orinoco. To the south, their occurrence has been noted as far as Madre de Dios in Peru and Beni in northern Bolivia, where the valleys of the Amazon tributaries offer living space. The favorite abodes of the Chestnut-fronted Macaws in Brazil, Venezuela, Guyana, Suriname, and French Guiana are the palm and virgin forests along rivers and overgrown tropical swamps up to altitudes of 600 m.

In some settled areas of their range, as a result of the expansion of agricultural fields through burning and lumbering, one can detect a noticeable population decline. In some areas, such as north and west of the Panama Canal Zone, the birds have

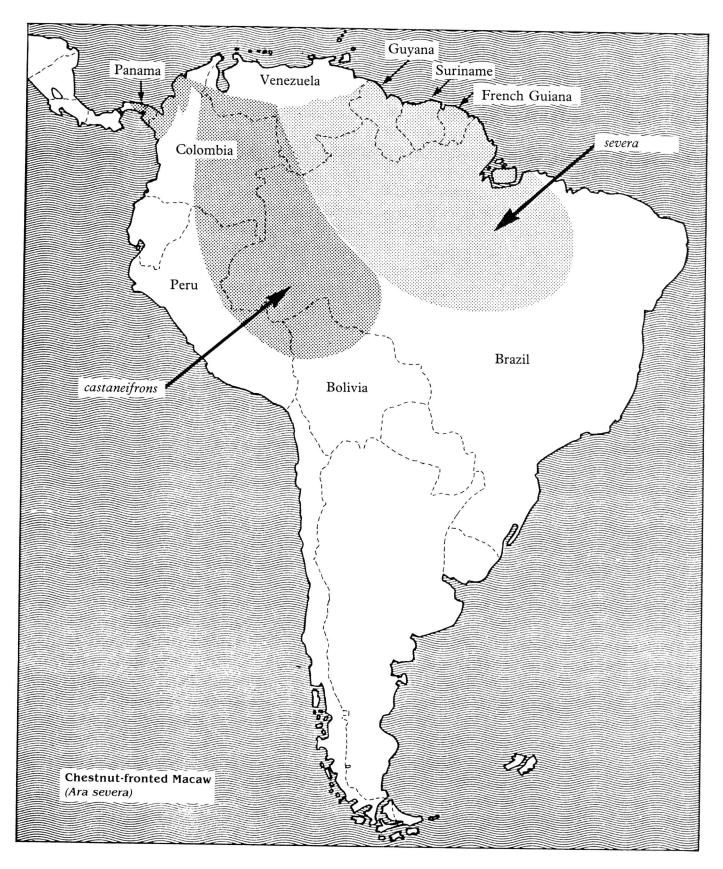

Panama

Venezuela

Guyana

Suriname

French Guiana

severa

Colombia

Peru

castaneifrons

Bolivia

Brazil

Chestnut-fronted Macaw
(Ara severa)

The Red-bellied Macaw (*Ara manilata*) is a dietary specialist, habitually consuming only the fruits of buriti palms (*Mauritia* sp.). Thus it differs markedly from other macaw species, which one can characterize as being generalists in their choice of food. Because of its differentiated nutritional preferences, it is difficult for it to adjust to the conditions of captivity.

1, 4. Prior to 1970, the Yellow-collared Macaw *(Ara auricollis)* was very rare among parrot fanciers. Afterward, however, it was imported frequently, and so a good captive stock of this species has been built up. 2. In the Walsrode bird park, these Blue-and-yellow Macaws are kept in the open throughout the day, from spring until fall. 3, 6. The Blue-throated Macaw *(Ara glaucogularis)* is one of the rarest parrots. Until a few years ago there was great doubt at as to the separate status of this species, since it was originally classified as a subspecies of the Blue-and-yellow Macaw *(Ara ararauna)*. 5. A Chestnut-fronted Macaw *(Ara severa)* in a typical posture of repose.

93

not been found for a long time and thus may have already died out there.

In the southern part of their range the breeding season of the Chestnut-fronted Macaw begins about November; in northern areas it shifts to the following months. Up to five eggs may be laid, approximately 38 x 30 mm. in size, which are incubated for approximately twenty-six to twenty-eight days. The chicks leave the nest after about seventy days but are still fed by the parents for a time afterwards.

P. Roth (pers. comm.) has described the breeding season in the Rio Aripuanã area:

The breeding season in this region lasts from the beginning of November to the end of January. In a dead branch of a tree 30 m. high standing in a clearing, *Ara severa* occupied a nest hole at a height of 23 m. in January. It was visited regularly and probably contained young.

In November of the same year (1978) it was noted that two Chestnut-fronted Macaws occupied a nest hole at a height of 28 m. in a brazil-nut tree. The diameter of the tree was more than 150 cm. at this height. On December 24, the tree was climbed and the nest inspected. Two chicks and a damaged egg were found. The older chick was about three weeks old, while the other was about four to six days younger. In the same tree we also found burrows made by tree termites. These holes had been selected as breeding places earlier by two to four pairs of Golden-winged Parakeets (*Brotgeris chrysopterus chrysosema*). A nest hole located about 1.2 m. under the "macaw hole" was occupied a short time later by a pair of White-eyed Conures (*Aratinga leucophthalmus*).

Care and Breeding. Chestnut-fronted Macaws are occasionally imported in the animal trade and offered at relatively favorable prices (the subspecies *A. s. severa* and *A. s. castaneifrons* are offered for the same price). Since there are no color differences between the races, it is best to ask the importer about the provenance of the animals. The slight difference in size between the geographic races does not permit an accurate determination. The author has owned several Chestnut-fronted Macaws and can confirm that these small parrots quickly become confiding. One even showed itself to be a gifted talker, with several Spanish words in its repertoire, and quickly learned a few German words as well as amazon screeches, unfortunately. Chestnut-fronted

Macaws kept singly soon attach themselves to their owner and can become very tame.

The first documented captive breeding of the Chestnut-fronted Macaw occurred in 1940 at the zoological garden in San Diego, U.S.A. Karl Neunzig (1921) reports that a breeder named Sharland had a pair of Chestnut-fronted Macaws that bred, but due to a thunderstorm the embryos died in the eggs. This pair is said to have bred a second time, but, unfortunately, Neunzig does not note how successful the second breeding was. In Europe, the first recorded captive breeding occurred in Copenhagen in 1954. After a nestling period of eight weeks, a youngster fledged and was still fed by its parents for six weeks longer. In 1958, the same breeding pair reared four young from five eggs. In 1964 in Germany, K. Oehler achieved a hybrid breeding between Illiger's Macaw (*Ara maracana*) and the Chestnut-fronted Macaw. Incubation should take twenty-three to twenty-four days (?) and the nestling period about six weeks (?).

Yellow-collared Macaw
Ara auricollis
Cassin 1853

Characteristics. Size, about 38 cm. Dark green. Forehead and crown greenish brown black. Occiput bluish green. Blackish green feathers bordering the lower bare cheek region. Nape band golden yellow. Primaries blue. Outer vanes of outer secondaries blue. Underside of wing green. Tail feathers brownish red, blue toward the tip. Underside of tail feathers olive green. Bare eye-cheek area yellowish white. Iris reddish brown. Beak black, upper mandible grayish toward the tip. Toes light flesh color. Female like the male, golden yellow nape band possibly a bit narrower. Young birds like adults, but lighter green. Nape band more yellowish, less distinct; sometimes scattered yellow feathers on the breast and belly.

Range. Southeastern Rondonia and Mato Grosso (Brazil). Western Paraguay. From Beni in northeastern Bolivia southward east of the Andes to northeastern Salta and possibly northwestern Formosa (Argentina).

Yellow-collared Macaw
(Ara auricollis)

1. Yellow-collared Macaw *(Ara auricollis)* resting: plumage slightly fluffed and one foot drawn up into the belly feathers. **2.** Macaws on a stand in a pet shop, such as this Military Macaw *(Ara militaris)* have been significant in awakening public interest in birds. **3.** The Red-shouldered Macaw *(Diopsittaca nobilis)* is the smallest species in all four macaw genera. Its strongly compressed lower mandible clearly shows the transition to the *Aratinga* species.

Way of Life. The range of the Yellow-collared Macaw embraces the most varied landscapes in the interior of the South American continent. In Brazil these small green macaws occur in the Mato Grosso highlands in the Federative State of Mato Grosso. Gomez told the author in 1978 that the western tributaries of the Paraná and the swamp areas of the Araguaia to the east form the natural boundaries of the range. According to Gomez, the Yellow-collared Macaws live in the gallery forests of the river valleys and their swamps. The macaws forage daily in the thornbush savannas, which lie beyond the river valleys.

The range extends westward to the eastern foothills of the Andes in the Bolivian departments of Beni, northeastern Cochabamba, Santa Cruz, eastern Chuquisca, and eastern Tarija. In parts of their Bolivian range the macaws occur from time to time in the dry savannas, but they are also to be found in great numbers in the virgin forest areas along the Rio Mamoré, the Rio Blanco, and Iténés/Guaporé and their tributaries. To the southwest, the birds are found as far as northeastern Salta in Argentina. In Paraguay the Yellow-collared Macaws live in the vast marshy area of the western Paraguayan lowlands. Small flocks of these macaws also occur in the hot, dry chaco area in western Paraguay.

Except for the breeding season, Yellow-collared Macaws exhibit the same party and flock behavior as most other species of macaws. Gomez saw flocks of up to 500 specimens congregated in sleeping trees. Small parties of six to twenty birds kept coming from all directions. Quarrels over the best perches ensued, with shrill screaming that constantly began anew. Fighting over perches continued a long time after darkness fell. In the early morning hours, shortly after dawn, small groups began to leave their roosts to go off together to search for food. Palm fruits and figs are essential and probably the main element of daily nourishment. They do not, however, spurn leaf and plant buds.

At the beginning of the breeding season, adult pairs separate from the colony. In the southern part of their range, courtship begins a short time after the beginning of the rainy season. Eggs are laid at two-day intervals. The clutch is complete early in December; as a rule, three eggs are laid. To the north, the beginning of the breeding season shifts a few weeks, but starts at the beginning of January at the latest. The cocks probably take part in incubating the eggs. The breeding season lasts twenty-seven to twenty-eight days, the nestling period of the chicks about ten to eleven weeks.

Care and Breeding. Until recently, Yellow-collared Macaws were an absolute rarity in the collections of parrot fanciers. Only a few zoos and bird parks were able to show these animals to the public in their exhibit areas. In Germany prior to 1970 these macaws were probably not even listed in any animal collection. Those specimens occasionally imported into Germany early in the 1970s were considered a one-time rarity, and the price asked was correspondingly high. A short time later, Yellow-collared Macaws appeared frequently in the trade, so that it became possible for a number of fanciers to acquire these interesting parrots.

As the author has kept some Yellow-collared Macaws, he can confirm that the animals become tame very quickly. Even though they were kept in a flock (which at times numbered more than ten), after a short acclimation period they took tidbits from the hand. A macaw kept in an indoor flight was so tame after one week that it allowed itself to be held. Its greatest pleasure was to be laid on its back and have its belly scratched. Its tameness was almost a problem, because it was nearly impossible to get the bird off one's shoulder. It was far more reserved toward women and would put up with them only if no men were available as "playmates." In learning to mimic sounds, whistles, or words, it was totally ungifted and showed no talent for talking. On the other hand, many Yellow-collared Macaws kept singly are very gifted talkers. The author has seen some Yellow-collared Macaws which as house pets took part in family life and had an extensive repertoire of words and whistles. Even when Yellow-collared Macaws are tame, they screech quite often. Frequently, without any apparent reason, they will raise their voices and emit their shrill cries. If the macaws are kept in an outdoor flight or on a balcony or terrace, one must hope for tolerant neighbors, because the macaws announce daybreak with joyful cries. Not every neighbor, even if he is otherwise a great lover of birds, will have the desired degree of understanding for another person's noisy hobby.

The best accommodations for Yellow-collared Macaws are outdoor flights with adjoining shelters that have windows with shutters or jalousies, so the rooms can be darkened. One should not keep Yellow-collared Macaws together with other species of parrots. The author had some unpleasant experiences in this way. Their aggressive behavior towards other bird species makes it advisable to keep them only with their own kind. Their flight should always be separated from adjacent ones by double wire mesh.

The first breeding of the Yellow-collared Macaw in Germany occurred in the aviaries of Klaus Maass. Herr Maass told the author that he obtained two Yellow-collared Macaws in January 1976. The birds were put into the aviary. While renovating the aviary complex, an egg was found in the nest box on July 10, 1978. Two days later a second egg was laid. After an incubation period of twenty-seven days, a chick was hatched on August 6, 1978. But three to four hours after the hatching, the chick inexplicably vanished. The nest box was abandoned and the second egg no longer incubated.

In 1979 the macaw pair was transferred into a smaller aviary. By May 19th, both macaws were ensconced in the nest box, a tree trunk 70 cm. high and 35 cm. in diameter. Inspection of the nest on June 3 revealed three eggs. Now the nest box was sprayed every day with up to a liter of water in order to raise the humidity inside the nest box. On June 26, 27, and 28, begging cries were heard for the first time and confirmed that the chicks had hatched. Inspection of the nest box was now out of the question, because upon entering the aviary the birds immediately began to attack. Banding or even photographing the young at this point was absolutely impossible. After the middle of August, the little macaws now and then showed themselves at the entrance hole of the nest box, and in their eleventh week they left the nest.

In 1980, there was another successful breeding of these Yellow-collared Macaws. The first 1980 attempt went awry in the course of aviary repairs, but from the second breeding two chicks hatched. The young differed from the adult birds only in their slightly lighter green color, smaller yellow neckband, and some yellow feathers in the breast plumage. During the breeding season, in addition to the usual parrot mixture, Herr Maass offered a rearing-food mixture consisting of one egg, two tablespoons of honeyed baby cereal, one tablespoon of bread crumbs, one tablespoon of cooked rice, two tablespoons of cooked corn, two tablespoons of dog chow (Latz-Hunde-Fertigfutter) a half teaspoon of dextrose powder, one and one-half teaspoons of pureed carrots with egg yolk (Alete brand) and two medium-sized crushed carrots.

Another successful breeding of Yellow-collared Macaws took place in 1978 in Switzerland. In the United States these birds were raised successfully in 1968. The first successful English breeding of Yellow-collared Macaws took place in the zoological garden in Bristol, where two offspring were reared.

In 1981, three Yellow-collared Macaws were raised in the aviary of a north German bird fancier named Ploog. From a group of four macaws, the breeding pair segregated themselves. The other two birds were also compatible, so it was hoped that, since three infertile eggs had been laid, there was another pair in the group. In spring of 1981, courtship and one treading were observed, and soon thereafter the hen disappeared into the nest log (100 cm. high, 30 cm. in diameter). Inspection of the nest log in May revealed three fertile eggs. The first youngster hatched on June 5; the others hatched five and eleven days later, respectively. This relatively long hatching interval probably stems from less tight incubation in the first days after egg laying. The chicks were reared without complications, and on August 13 the oldest chick left the nest. Thus the nestling period lasted sixty-nine days. Soon after, the other two young birds followed. The young macaws were fed by their parents for a month after leaving the nest.

Blue-headed Macaw
Ara couloni
Sclater 1876

Characteristics. Size, about 41 cm. Green. Forecrown and cheeks blue. Occiput turquoise blue. Breast and belly olive green. Primaries and outer secondaries blue. Outer greater wing coverts blue.

Blue-headed Macaw
(Ara couloni)

Peru

Brazil

Carpal edge blue. Upper side of tail feathers red brown, blue toward the tip. Underside of tail yellow green. Iris yellow. Restricted bare eye-cheek region gray blue. Beak black, light horn color on the ridge of the tip. Toes flesh color. Female probably like the male. Young birds probably like adults.

Range. Central part of the province of Loreto in Peru. Extreme western parts of the provinces of Amazonas and Acre in Brazil.

Remarks. In 1876, Dr. P. L. Sclater received a skin of a Blue-headed Macaw from Paul-Louis de Coulon and in his honor named the macaw after him. De Coulon (1804–1894) was the director of the natural-history museum in Neuchatel, Switzerland.

Some ornithologists regard the Blue-headed Macaw as a subspecies of Illiger's Macaw (*Ara maracana*), the range of which lies to the east and southeast of the range of the Blue-headed Macaw. The differences between the two species leaves absolutely no doubt about their distinctness.

Way of Life. The Blue-headed Macaw is endemic to the partly unexplored virgin forests of La Montaña, located to the east of the Eastern Cordilleras in Peru, an area which seldom reaches altitudes of 500 m. One supposes that the range of this rare macaw is bounded in the north by the Huallaga and Marañón rivers. In the west, the eastern foothills of the Eastern Cordilleras in the valleys of the Apurimac and the Ucayali form the boundary of its natural living space. The Cordillera de Dios and the Brazilian frontier are the boundaries of the range of the Blue-headed Macaw in the south and east.

We have no details as yet of the life of the Blue-headed Macaw in the wild. Although nowadays, even in unsettled eastern Peru, bulldozers have obtained a foothold in the gigantic Amazon virgin forest, the range of the Blue-headed Macaw is still a blank spot on the map. The huge tracts of virgin forest are impassable not only in the rainy season, October to May; even during the dry season—if one can speak of a dry season—this area cannot be penetrated in ordinary fashion. The extreme heat combined with almost hundred-percent humidity completely discourages the spirit of exploration after only a few meters have been traversed. This

probably also explains the extremely scant field observations of these birds. O'Neill (1969) reports that on the river Curanja at Balta, in an area 300 m. above sea level, the macaws could be observed in pairs and in groups of threes. In the range of the Blue-headed Macaw the rainy season lasts from October through April. It is not known to what extent the macaws adjust their breeding season to the rainy season. It is quite conceivable that the mating, incubation, and nestling periods do occur between October and April. The nestling period of the young probably lasts two months, as it does with related species of small macaws.

Care and Breeding. There are very few reports about maintaining the Blue-headed Macaw and none at all about breeding it in captivity. Information about this bird in the wild is just as sparse as information about its life in captivity. It is likely that the very rare Blue-headed Macaw first arrived in Germany just before World War I, as it was represented in the collection of the Berlin Zoo at this time. An American, David West, is probably one of the few fanciers who have had the opportunity to keep a Blue-headed Macaw (a male) in captivity. Even Walsrode and the well-known zoological garden in San Diego were unable to obtain these rare animals. Even in its range, according to R. S. Ridgely (1980), it is not kept as a cage bird by the local populace.

A skin of the Blue-headed Macaw is in the collection of the Senckenberg Museum in Frankfurt am Main. The bird was collected on November 18, 1961, in the tropical rainforest on the Rio Pachitea (a tributary of the Ucayali), at Hacienda Flor, near Puerto Victoria, about 350 m. above sea level. Sex: male; weight: 267.0 g.; length: 39.5 cm.; wing: 24.0 cm.

Illiger's Macaw
Ara maracana
(Vieillot 1816)

Characteristics. Size, about 43 cm. Green. Forehead red. Forecrown and crown, throat, neck, and breast bluish green. Red V-shaped patch on the belly between the thighs. Lower back red. Primaries blue. Secondaries and greater wing coverts blue green, edged with yellowish green. Underside of wings olive green. Tail feathers red brown, blue toward the tip. Underside of tail feathers yellowish green. Bare eye-cheek region whitish, and lightly marked with very thin lines of dark feathers. Iris orange brown. Toes light flesh color. Female like the male, but areas of red feathering less extensive and more orange red. Young birds like adults, but paler; red areas less extensive.

Range. Brazil: southeastern Pará, southern Maranhão, southern Piauí, western Pernambuco, Bahia, Goiás, eastern Mato Grosso, Minas Gerais, São Paulo, Paraná, Santa Catarina, and northern Rio Grande do Sul. Eastern Paraguay. Misiones in Argentina.

Way of Life. The range of Illiger's Macaw encompasses the Brazilian Highlands as well as a part of the highlands of the Mato Grosso. In the north the range ends right where the Amazon lowlands, rich in virgin forest, begin. Great parts of the range of Illiger's Macaw are being exploited for agriculture and lumber, as well as industrially, with the result that the macaws have already been forced out of much of their natural living space; in some places they have already died out. The birds have been driven out of the thickly populated Atlantic coastal strip in particular and forced into the backcountry.

Although the Brazilian Highlands form a single entity in terms of geological origin, quite diverse landscapes have arisen in the course of time. The northern part of the Highlands, which at the same time forms the northern boundary of this macaw's range, is a tropical landscape which is dominated by irregular rainfall: hot, dry scrubland characterizes the biotope. The western range of these macaws, which continues into the highlands of the Mato Grosso, is a similar landscape, interrupted by gallery forest only along the rivers. The southern part of the range, in the states of Rio Grande do Sul, Santa Catarina, Paraná, and São Paulo, is characterized by huge forests, which to a great extent have already been sacrificed to progress and have had to give way to agricultural pursuits. Generally, the southeastern part of the range of

Illiger's Macaw is very densely populated and covered with many industrial areas; thus it is to be feared that in the near future the birds will have disappeared completely from this region.

Gomez told the author that in the early 1960s he could still see great flocks of these macaws in the countryside around São Paulo, but in recent years he has seen only small groups of twenty birds at most. In the vicinity of the falls of the Rio Iguaçu (at the river's mouth, 4 km. wide, 130–180 million m³ of water flow into the Rio Paraná over a precipice 80 m. high, making them the world's largest waterfalls), Illiger's Macaws are still common in the forest, according to Gomez. The region around Iquazu Falls, where the borders of Brazil, Argentina, and Paraguay meet, was declared a nature preserve, and it is assumed that the living space used by the birds will be kept intact in the future, and in its pristine state. In this protected area, late in December 1979, Gomez discovered a nest hole very high in a dead tree. Since the adult birds flew into the nest quite frequently, one may assume that chicks in there were being fed.

Forshaw (1973, 1977) reports that Illiger's Macaws are numerous in the northern part of their range and that their habitat includes forests along rivers.

The author was not able to learn any additional details about the breeding habits of these birds, but it is certain that the breeding season in the southern part of the range begins toward the end of October. This is confirmed by Gomez's observation. In the northern part of the range the beginning of the breeding season is shifted slightly by a few weeks, into the following month. The behavior of Illiger's Macaw is like that of related small macaw species and follows the same daily course.

Care and Breeding. Occasionally Illiger's Macaws can be found in the trade. Without exception, these birds come from Bolivia and Paraguay, since Brazil has completely cut off commercial trade in these animals. Illiger's Macaws are appealing charges that become tame relatively quickly and also show some talent for talking. They find it easiest to learn words with short syllables, beginning and ending with the letters *a* and *o*. In keeping a bird singly it is vital that the bird be kept constantly occupied or always

Brazil

Paraguay

Argentina

Illiger's Macaw
(Ara maracana)

in the company of people. This is true not only for Illiger's Macaw but also for any parrot kept as a single bird.

The first and most successful breeding took place at the London Zoo. Two chicks were reared in the parrot house in 1931. In the years which followed, the breeding pair almost regularly raised two chicks a year.

Since 1960 there have been isolated cases of successful breedings of Illiger's Macaws in some European countries as well as in the United States. These macaws generally began courtship in March or April. Some pairs shifted their breeding activity to January or even to the months of August and October. On most occasions, up to three and sometimes as many as five eggs were laid. The egg-laying interval was three days. Incubation by the hen began with the first egg laid, and the chicks hatched after an incubation period of twenty-six to twenty-seven days. According to reports from some of the breeders, the nestling period lasts about ninety days. To the author, the ninety-day nestling period stated seems too long for this small macaw species; seventy days seems more likely. Both parents fed the young birds.

Another successful breeding of Illiger's Macaw took place in the winter of 1980–1981 in Switzerland. E. Grünig obtained two pairs in 1976, which were kept together in one flight. After a year, there were attempts at mating but also fighting between the cocks, so the pairs had to be separated. Nest boxes were installed in both indoor flights of the aviary, and from the day that they were provided, the birds used them for sleeping. In 1979 one pair laid five eggs, but none of these were fertile. A short time later this pair was given to another breeder.

The second pair began breeding in the winter of 1979–1980, and four eggs were laid. During the morning hours the cock relieved the hen of incubation duties for a short time. Unfortunately, the eggs did not hatch, although three of them contained fully developed chicks, while the fourth was infertile. A short time later, there were two more clutches, but both were unsuccessful. As a result of this failure, the macaws were transferred to another flight in the hope that a "change of scene" would result in breeding attempts with a positive outcome. The indoor flight measured 80 x 150 x

100 cm.; the outdoor flight was 150 x 200 x 210 cm.

In December 1980, the Illiger's Macaws were busy all day going in and out of the limbawood nest box (25 x 28 x 50 cm.), and soon the female stayed inside. On January 15, 1981, the cock began climbing into the nest box several times a day, so there was hope that there might be a chick. On January 22, inspection revealed that the hen was sitting on two chicks and one infertile egg. During the initial period, the cock fed both the hen and the chicks. After the young birds were three weeks old, the hen again began to feed herself. The chicks grew splendidly and left the nest on March 19, 1981. For a long time after their fledging, the entire family would spend the night in the nest box.

F. Veser of Tettnang owns one of the most successful breeding pairs. His Illiger's Macaws are kept in an aviary with an indoor flight 2.6 x 1.2 x 2.0–2.5 m. high, and an outdoor flight 4.0 x 1.2 x 1.8 m. high. In between 1974 and 1981, the macaw pair raised forty-nine youngsters:

1974	1 breeding	3 young
1975	1 breeding	3 young
1976	2 breedings	4 + 3 young
1977	2 breedings	4 + 3 young
1978	2 breedings	4 + 3 young
1979	2 breedings	4 + 3 young
1980	2 breedings	4 + 3 young
1981	2 breedings	4 + 4 young

This pair was about five years old when purchased in the fall of 1973. The male has a somewhat more extensive red abdominal patch. The birds weigh 250 g.; there is no difference in weight between male and female.

Just a half year after their purchase the macaws occupied a nest box with an interior diameter of 25 cm. and an interior height of 52 cm.; the entrance hole had a diameter of 8.5 cm. The nest box was also gnawed, yet it suited the macaw pair despite its small size. In every breeding, this nest box was used by the birds. Egg laying followed at intervals of one-and-a-half to two days, with up to five eggs laid. The size of the eggs was about 33 x 25 mm. The eggs are tightly incubated after the first egg, and the chicks hatch after an incubation period of twenty-four days (says Veser), according to the laying intervals. The male does not participate in incubation, but he always perches at the entrance hole and stands guard.

A few days after hatching, the flesh-colored bodies of the chicks become covered with white down. The beak, which in the first days of life is a light horn color, likewise begins to change color. At first the lower mandible becomes dark, then the upper, which changes color from bottom to top. The ridge of the upper mandible is light for a longer time, but by the time of fledging it also has become black. The tip of the upper mandible becomes dark at the latest a few days after leaving the nest. Feather sheaths break through first on the head, wings, and tail, and soon the feather colors are completely recognizable. The toes, which during the first days are flesh colored, become dark gray; only after the bird leaves the nest do they take on their final coloration. The development of the orange red forehead is quite variable. After just a few weeks some chicks already show a deeply colored spot on the forehead, while others have only scattered orange red feathers or just blue green feathers on the forehead.

The parent birds never resented inspection of the nest box. As soon as the aviary was entered, the cock would join the female and the chicks in the nest box. When it was opened for inspection, the entire group laid on their backs and screamed murderously. Adjacent flights were separated by double wiring because the Illiger's Macaws were very aggressive toward the occupants.

The nestling period lasts about two months (however, other breeders cite longer periods). After leaving the nest, the chicks from the second breeding are still fed for three months by the parents. The first brood of chicks are removed from the flight six to eight weeks after leaving the nest, as soon as the parents begin to breed again.

Veser offers his Illiger's Macaws the following food mixture: parrot mix; CéDé® nestling food with one mashed hard-boiled egg, including the shell, and mixed with edible calcium; sprouted sunflower seed; rose hips (from the freezer); half-ripe corn; plenty of fruit and carrots; and, in the winter, greens and a constant supply of branches from fresh fruit trees. Once a week a multivitamin, such as Multimulsin® or Nekton-S®, is added to the drinking water. During breeding, the CéDé®,

sprouted sunflower seed, and greens are given in larger quantities.

Red-bellied Macaw
Ara manilata
(Boddaert 1783)

Characteristics. Size, about 48 cm. Green. Forehead and forecrown blue, becoming green on the occiput. Back and belly feathers edged with greenish yellow. Breast feathers bluish green, edged with greenish yellow. Dark red brown spot on the lower belly. Thigh feathers bluish green, with light edges. Small red brown band of feathers at the end of the thighs. Primaries dark blue, inner vanes edged blue black. Outer vanes of secondaries blue. Outer vanes of outer greater wing coverts greenish blue. Underside of wings yellow green. Upper tail coverts blue green. Tail feathers green. Underside of tail feathers yellow green. Bare facial zone yellowish. Iris brown. Beak black. Toes dark gray. Female probably like the male. Young birds like adults, but dark red brown belly spot less extensive.

Range. Trinidad. Southwestward through northeastern and southern Venezuela and eastern Colombia to northeastern Peru. Eastward through the Guianas to Piauî (Brazil). Southward to northern Mato Grosso, northern Goiás, and western Bahia (Brazil).

Way of Life. Although the Red-bellied Macaw is quite common in the wild and has an extensive range, only meager details about its behavior are available. The author was able to observe Red-bellied Macaws many times in Trinidad and Guyana, but never in the company of Amazons. Herklots (1961), on the other hand, was able to see Red-bellied Macaws flying with Orange-winged Amazons (*Amazona amazonica*). On Trinidad these macaws occur in all types of country up to the highlands of the Northern Range and are found even in the city park of Port of Spain. The mangrove swamps in the east, south, and west serve the birds as sleeping places. During the day the birds fly off into the hilly, open backcountry. Since the author has visited Guyana and Trinidad only in

Trinidad
Guyana
Suriname
French Guiana

Venezuela

Colombia

Peru

Brazil

Red-bellied Macaw
(Ara manilata)

the early summer (breeding season), it was never possible for him to observe flocks of these interesting animals. In 1961 Herklots claimed that the population of Red-bellied Macaws had increased on Trinidad. Today, however, this information is no longer accurate. With the spread of industrial areas in the western coastal regions, new oil fields opening up in the interior, and expanding agriculture, the living space of the macaws has been sharply limited. Residents have told this author that the population of Red-bellied Macaws has declined markedly in recent years and outside the breeding season large flocks of the birds are seldom seen. Thus our "new age" exacts its tribute. In the eastern part of the island, on Cocos Bay, the author discovered two nests in dead coconut palms about 100 m. apart. The nest holes were about 10 m. above the ground. It is interesting that the nesting trees stood some 80 m. away from the edge of the Atlantic.

As a rule, the mating season begins in February in the Guianas, northeastern Venezuela, and Trinidad, so that the young have fledged before the rainy season, which in these latitudes often begins in the middle of May, and frequently earlier. The fruits of the mauritia palms (*Mauritia flexuosa*) serve as food for the Red-bellied Macaws throughout their range. Where these palms are numerous, Red-bellied Macaws are also usually present.

In Guyana, Suriname, and French Guiana, the macaws live in the coastal strip, a hot and humid lowland, fifteen to twenty kilometers wide, interspersed with mangrove swamps, and also in the savanna "islands" of the interior, which lie in the rain shadow of the highland rainforests. In the inaccessible coastal backcountry of the Guianas, which can be reached only by small airplanes since penetration via a land route is almost impossible, field observation becomes very difficult. Surely, in these unexplored regions there are still many botanical and zoological puzzles to solve.

In Venezuela their range encompasses the southeastern part of the country. Meyer de Schauensee and Phelps report that the Red-bellied Macaws are found from sea level to as high as 500 m., and that they populate swamp areas, such as the Orinoco Delta, and riverine forests. North of the Orinoco, with the exception of the Orinoco Delta, the macaws are absent. Even in Venezuela the fruits

of the mauritia palms are the main food of the animals. In southeastern Colombia and northeastern Peru, Red-bellied Macaws prefer the same sort of country as they do in Venezuela.

In northern Brazil the animals live exclusively in the Amazonian lowlands, which extend from the mouth of the mighty river (which is 200 km. wide), to Peru, Colombia, and Bolivia. The highlands of Mato Grosso and the Brazilian Highlands and their foothills are the boundaries of the range to the north and west. The range of the Red-bellied Macaw clearly indicates that these birds are purely tropical-lowland inhabitants found only in humid regions. They are not present in hot, dry areas north of the Orinoco, such as Llanos del Orinoco or in the highlands of the Mato Grosso.

The usual course of the Red-bellied Macaws' day corresponds to that of other macaw species. In the early morning hours, small flocks, seldom more than ten birds, leave their sleeping places to search for food. During the flight, shrill cries are uttered, but as soon as the birds have settled in trees or palms, they quiet down and only soft chatter is heard. During the day the animals mostly stay in the vicinity of the food trees. Meanwhile, feathers are thoroughly preened, and a midday nap is taken. A little rain is often the occasion for a thorough "shower bath." In the late afternoon hours they make the return flight to the sleeping trees. Without exception, the sleeping trees stand in swampland or on small islands in rivers, locations which offer a safe haven from enemies.

P. Roth notes that the buriti palms (*Mauritia* sp.) do not all fruit simultaneously, so that in a large area there are supplies of fruit to be had at every season. Therefore, there is always a steady supply of food within the flight range of the Red-bellied Macaws.

In the southernmost part of their range, the Amazon lowlands, the breeding season starts in January. In areas to the north, it begins in February and March. According to Herklots (1961), two eggs are laid; abandoned woodpecker holes or cavities in palms and trees serve as nesting places. No data are available on the duration of the incubation and nestling periods, but it may be assumed that there are no essential differences from the other small macaw species, such as, for example, the Chestnut-fronted Macaw (*Ara severa*).

In Aripuanā, in the border region between Mato Grosso and Amazonas, P. Roth has observed that, beginning in September, Red-bellied Macaw flocks consisting of about 150 individuals broke up; by December and January they had decreased to a low of twenty. The sexually mature pairs had separated from the flock by this time and had spread out in order to devote themselves to breeding activities. They rejoined the flock in February, with youngsters. Pairs that did not complete breeding came back sooner.

Care and Breeding. The German name *Rotbauchara* ("Red-bellied Macaw") is probably not very aptly chosen. Illiger's Macaw (*Ara maracana*) is often called red-bellied because it has a V-shaped red patch on its lower belly; the name Red-bellied Macaw would be more appropriate for it. Since the stores specializing in animals very rarely offer small macaws for sale, fanciers turn to ads in specialist bird periodicals. Before embarking on a long journey to a seller, one should telephone or write in advance to precisely determine which animal is offered, making sure of the coloration of its feathers. There are often name mixups with the small macaws, and it is very annoying after a trip of a couple of hundred kilometers to discover that the species actually for sale is not the species one wishes to acquire.

The Red-bellied Macaw is seldom imported. Animal dealers in Trinidad and Guyana explained to the author that the Red-bellied Macaws are very difficult to maintain and are very susceptible to illness during the acclimation period. Similar statements have been made by German and English fanciers who have kept these little macaws in their stock, confirming that all Red-bellied Macaws are very sensitive to changes in temperature. Colds appear in the birds as soon as the temperature falls below 20 C. Even during the height of summer it was impossible to keep the birds in an outdoor aviary, because even slight variations in temperature could bring on colds and respiratory infections. Ideal housing for Red-bellied Macaws is a well-lit indoor flight. The daytime temperature should be at least 25 C., and it should not fall below 20 C. at night. The humidity should be 80% or higher. Since such temperatures and humidity levels foster the growth of fungus, regular care and cleaning of the enclosure (daily, if possible) is a prerequisite for keeping the birds healthy.

As already mentioned, Red-bellied Macaws are seldom found in the possession of bird fanciers, although they are numerous in the wild. Importers are probably afraid to import the birds because of their susceptibility to illness. Fanciers who intend to acquire these beautiful macaws should make absolutely sure that they will be housed in a natural fashion; i.e., proper climatic conditions are absolutely essential to the well-being of the animals, and only by providing them will losses be prevented. According to T. Silva (pers. comm.), an American, G. Harrison of Florida, has been successful in breeding *Ara manilata*.

Military Macaw
Ara militaris
(Linnaeus 1766)

Three subspecies:

1. *Ara militaris militaris* (Linnaeus)

Characteristics. Size, about 70 cm. Olive green. Forehead and lores carmine red. Head green. Throat brownish green. Primaries and secondaries blue. Underside of wings green yellow. Lower back and upper tail coverts blue. Tail feathers brownish red, blue toward the tip. Bare facial area whitish pink traversed with lines of black green feathers, above the eyes lines of reddish feathers. Iris yellowish. Beak black. Toes dark gray. Female like the male, but head somewhat more slender. Young birds like adults; iris brownish.

Range. From northwestern Zulia (Venezuela) and southern Guajira (Colombia) southward to northeastern Ecuador. The provinces of Lambeyeque and Cajamarca in Peru.

2. *Ara militaris mexicana* Ridgway

Characteristics. Like the nominate subspecies, but noticeably larger.

Range. Central Mexico from southeastern Sonora and southwestern Chihuahua southward to the Isthmus of Tehuantepec; from southern Nuevo Leon and southern Tamaulipas southward to the province of México.

3. *Ara militaris boliviana* Reichenow

Characteristics. Like the nominate subspecies, but somewhat larger. Throat more red brown. Feathers at the ear region reddish at the base. More intense blue on the primaries and at the tip of the tail.

Range. East of the Andes in southeastern Bolivia and eastern Jujuy and northern Salta in Argentina.

Remarks. It is highly questionable whether the species *Ara militaris* and *Ara ambiqua* are actually separate forms (see also "Remarks" on *Ara ambigua*).

In 1939, another subspecies of the Military Macaw was described by A. J. van Rossem and Marquess Hachisuka and named *Ara militaris sheffleri*. This geographical race cannot be recognized, since a type-specimen, as stipulated by zoological nomenclature, was not designated.

Way of Life. The three races of the Military Macaw prefer to live in dry country. The leeward hillsides of the dry subtropical and temperate zones up to altitudes of 2500 m., with deciduous, oak, and pine forests, are ideal habitat for Military Macaws. The author holds the opinion that the Military Macaw is found primarily at altitudes above 800 m. It is quite conceivable that in their flights for food the birds also appear in lowland areas, but generally they occupy only higher regions. Indeed, Phelps and Phelps (1958) report that they had encountered these macaws frequently in the tropical-zone forests of Colombia and northwestern Venezuela; this author suspects, however, that the birds appear in these forest zones only briefly in their daily forays for food. Ramirez informed the author that he found Military Macaws in northeastern Colombia only at altitudes above 1000 m.; at no season could he find the birds in more low-lying country. On the other hand, Ramirez saw Great Green Macaws in forested river valleys of the lower western slopes of the Cordillera Occidental at altitudes up to 500 m. In higher regions in Colombia only the Military Macaw occurs.

As mentioned earlier, in Colombia Military Macaws are found only in the higher montane valleys. The Rio Magdalena and its tributaries, which drain the eastern slopes of the Cordillera Central and the western slopes of the Cordillera Oriental; the eastern and western slopes of the Sierra de Perijá, which separates Colombia and Venezuela; the slopes of the Sierra Nevada de Santa Marta, with the 5775-meter-high Pico Christobal Colon; and the mountain valleys of the Aquarico (a tributary of the Amazon) in northern Equador — these are the boundaries of one of the segments of the range of this macaw.

In northern Peru the geographical race *Ara militaris militaris* occurs locally on the slopes of the Cordillera Central in the department of Marañón. Apparently, in September and October (Köpcke, 1963), the macaws fly into the montane forests of the Pacific bluffs; to do so, they must cross over areas lying above the tree line.

The second geographical race, *Ara militaris mexicana*, likewise a highland bird, is found in Mexico chiefly in the mountains of the Sierra Madre Oriental and the Sierra Madre Occidental. After the breeding season, which in this range segment begins in April and May and ends when the young attain full independence in October and November, the birds wander into the Pacific and Caribbean coastal backcountry, at this time probably moving as far south as the Sierra Madre del Sur, which slopes toward the Isthmus of Tehuantepec in southeastern Oaxaca. In recent years, though, the macaws have no longer been seen in the state of Oaxaca. The author traveled in Mexico through a great part of the region in which these macaws occur. This segment of the range of the Military Macaw is climatically quite comparable to Central Europe, for example, the south side of the Alps or the slopes of the Pyrenees.

The Barranca del Cobre and the Barranca del Urique are canyons dug by the Urique river in the course of thousands of years to a depth of 1500 m., creating a spectacular landscape. In the higher regions of these canyons night frosts occur well into late spring and then again in early fall, as a rule. Snowfalls are not unusual, and even in early

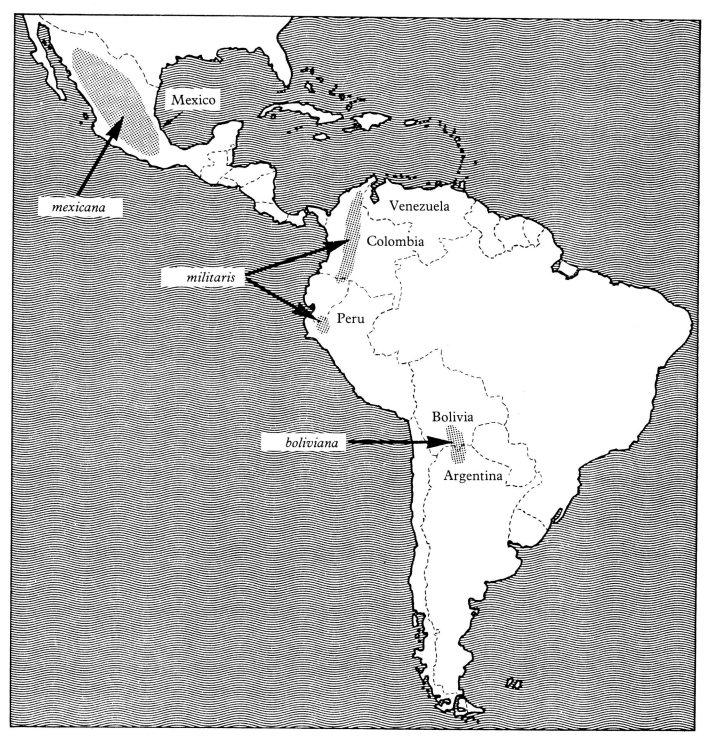

Military Macaw *(Ara militaris)*

summer temperatures at night can fall to zero C. On the other hand, at lower elevations in the *barrancas*, a drier, subtropical climate prevails. In these areas the native Indians, who live apart from all civilization, cultivate wheat and corn. The slopes are covered with scattered cacti, agaves, acacias, and mesquite bushes. In the lowest parts of the *barrancas*, banana and citrus trees are planted. In May 1976, in the Barranca del Cobre, from a great distance the author saw a solitary Military Macaw sitting in a fig tree. It was probably a male, keeping watch in the vicinity of a nest hole where a female was probably sitting on eggs.

In Mexico, Military Macaws live in inaccessible mountain valleys which are often covered with pine and oak forests. In this range segment their breeding season begins in the dry months of April and May. The young birds then fledge in the rainy season, which starts sometime around the end of June. Only in the autumn months, when the chicks are fully independent, do family units assemble in small flocks of up to twenty animals. Outside the breeding season, the birds in Mexico are probably constantly wandering, traversing large areas in search of food. The birds return to their former nesting areas at the start of the breeding season.

Ara militaris mexicana exhibits a close relationship to the genus of thick-billed parrots (*Rhynchopsitta*).

No information about the way of life of *A. m. boliviana* is available. However, one may assume that the behavior and habits of these macaws are identical to those of the two northern races. This subspecies lives in the Andean valleys of southeastern Bolivia and the Argentine provinces of eastern Jujuy and northern Salta.

The breeding season of *boliviana* begins in November or December; that of *mexicana* in April to June, and that of the nominate subspecies in January to March. Up to three eggs are laid and incubated by the female for twenty-five to twenty-six days. The nestling period of the youngsters lasts about three months.

Care and Breeding. The Military Macaw seldom appears in the trade. It is for sale somewhat more often than its close relative, the Great Green Macaw (*Ara ambigua*); nevertheless, it is a rarity in the hands of fanciers. Since the macaws occur only locally in their range, in small numbers in out-of-

the-way places, only a few birds come into the trade. When they occasionally are offered for sale, the price for this species is half again as high, for example, as for the Blue-and-yellow Macaw (*Ara ararauna*) or the Scarlet Macaw (*Ara macao*).

In regard to housing and feeding, the Military Macaw has the same requirements as the other large macaw species, although the Military Macaw is much more able to withstand temperature fluctuations. After the acclimation period, the birds can be kept in an outdoor flight from March to November without concern, although in parts of the Military Macaw's range frost at night is quite common. The author refuses to keep the macaws out in the open in the winter. Obviously, on pleasant winter days one can permit the birds a midday outing in the outdoor flight, but they must always be able to return to the heated indoor flight.

Military Macaws have a relatively great talent for mimicry and are capable of learning whole sentences. Like all macaws, if kept singly, they view the person who regulary cares for them as their "mate."

Quite frequently there have been offspring from the Military Macaw. Of course, due to careless and inexact reports in the literature, there has always been confusion with the Great Green Macaw (*Ara ambigua*), so that in some accounts of successful breeding it cannot be said with certainty whether they refer to the Military or to the Great Green macaw. In some cases there have probably been hybrid offspring that were not recognized as such. It often seems that parrot fanciers disregard all taxonomic rules and give free rein to their imagination in giving names. An additional handicap which often leads to inaccurate species designation in these macaws is that in a great part of the English literature the two species are treated as one. It is certainly true that both species are very closely related and can be regarded as one species—and the author tends in this direction—but as long as the birds are treated as two distinct species in the currently valid check-list, then nomenclature should follow the valid list, in order to avoid confusion.

There is supposed to have been a hybrid breeding between a female Military Macaw and a male Scarlet Macaw (*Ara macao*) in the London Zoo in 1901. Successful pure breedings of the Military

Macaw took place at the zoo in Wellington, New Zealand, in 1973. Busch Gardens in Tampa, Florida, was able to raise a chick in a very small aviary in 1978. In Texas, over a period of several years, there have been hybrid breedings between a male Military Macaw and a female Scarlet Macaw (*Ara macao*) in the aviaries of a parrot fancier. Even the Tierpark in Berlin (GDR) reported a successful breeding of the Military Macaw. Since in recent years Military Macaws have been imported to West Germany in small numbers, one can hope that in the near future successful breedings will be reported here.

Great Green Macaw
Ara ambigua
(Bechstein 1811)

Two subspecies:

1. *Ara ambigua ambigua* (Bechstein)

Characteristics. Size, about 85 cm. Olive green. Forehead and lores red. Primaries and secondaries blue. Greater wing coverts edged with blue. Underside of wings light olive green. Lower back and upper tail coverts blue. Under tail coverts light blue. Tail red brown, blue toward the tip. Underside of tail light olive green, darker at the edges. Bare facial area pink traversed with closely spaced lines of black feathers. Lines of red feathers between the eye and lores. Iris yellowish. Beak black. Toes dark gray. Female like the male, but head more slender. Young birds like adults; iris brownish.

Range. From northeastern Nicaragua southward to Chocó in Colombia.

2. *Ara ambigua guayaquilensis* Chapman

Characteristics. Like the nominate subspecies, but undersides of wings and tail green.

Range. Western Ecuador northward to southwestern Colombia.

Remarks. It has not been possible to fully resolve the question of whether the Great Green Macaw and the Military Macaw are a single species or actually two distinct species. The author inclines toward the opinion that they are a single species. The distribution of *Ara ambigua* encompasses terrain up to 800 m. in altitude. *Ara militaris*, on the other hand, is found lower than 600 m. extremely infrequently and then only briefly on forays for food. The zone mainly used lies between altitudes of 600 and 2500 m. If one supposes that the Great Green Macaw and the Military Macaw should be treated as a single species, this yields an almost continuous range that extends from central Mexico to Ecuador.

Way of Life. The Republic of Honduras in Central America forms the northernmost boundary of the range of the Great Green Macaw. Columbus set foot on the coast of Honduras in 1502, during his fourth voyage, and therefore it was the first piece of land in Central America seen by Europeans. Honduras is divided into four landscape types. Great Green Macaws mainly inhabit the eastern lowlands, which are called the Costa de Mosquitos. In these low-lying plains—which give way to hilly highlands toward the west that merge into the Cordillera Isabelia and the Cordillera Chontalena—rainfall exceeds 3000 mm. per year, and as much as 5000 mm. on the eastern mountain slopes. The temperature stays about 25 C., with very high humidity. In the range of the Great Green Macaw (which is uncommon in Honduras), virgin tropical forest prevails, of which in recent years fifty percent has been burned clear for agriculture or cut down for lumber. Humid and dry savannas are found in the areas that formerly were virgin forest. Some ornithologists think that the Great Green Macaw has already died out in Honduras. In Costa Rica too the macaws occur in virgin forest. These macaws are found in the thinly populated Caribbean coastal belt, east of the Cordillera Central and the Cordillera de Talamanca, especially; and they also occur inland in the foothills of the cordilleras up to an altitude of 650 m. Great Green Macaws are seldom found on the Pacific coast in Costa Rica.

In Panama they have already been driven out of some parts of their range. R. S. Ridgely (1980) states that the birds disappeared completely from the Canal Zone some years ago. A population decline has also been reported from other parts of Panama, especially the western part of the narrow isthmus. East of the Panama Canal toward the Colombian border the macaws again become more common. The lowlands of Darién in particular, where virgin tropical forests, savannas, and mangrove swamps make a highly varied landscape, are the main stronghold of this large green macaw. In this hot, humid climate, these undeveloped, little-disturbed landscapes, barely touched by agriculture, are still for the macaws a natural biotope in pristine condition.

To the south, the range the Great Green Macaw continues into western Colombia. The delta at the mouth of the Atrato, with its great swampland, can certainly be designated the distributional core of these macaws. Further south, the range extends between the Pacific coast and the western foothills of the western cordillera (Cordillera Occidental) to the mouth of the Rio San Juan. With a hot, humid climate, the Pacific coastal region consists of tropical rainforest. The coastal belt, 20–40 km. wide, is edged with mangroves.

The subspecies *guayaquilensis* has an isolated range which begins in southwestern Colombia and extends to the Gulf of Guayaquil in Ecuador. The landscape varies according to the change in rainfall from north to south. Thus, in the northern part virgin coastal tropical forests are found; around the mouths of rivers mangrove swamps prevail; toward the south the landscape changes into moist savanna. This subspecies is extremely rare; a very small population dwells in the restricted range.

Both races of the Great Green Macaw are pure virgin-forest birds seldom found in open country. The strongly imprinted flocking behavior of other macaw species cannot be seen in the Great Green Macaw. For the most part, the birds roam through the forests in pairs or small family bands in search of food. Food is abundant in all parts of the range. Small, local migrations seldom need to be undertaken, so one can definitely characterize the

macaws as sedentary.

Ramirez told the author that in July and August, in the vicinity of Titumate, between the Golfo de Urabá and the Serranía del Darién, he saw bands of Great Green Macaws, up to five birds, flying above the treetops, always shortly after sunrise and before sunset. In the oblique morning and evening rays of the sun, the belly and undersides of the wings gleamed with a resplendent golden olive. The flapping wings were quiet and were not raised above the body; nevertheless, the macaws flew at a high speed. Rarely while in flight did they make loud cries. After the birds descended into the treetops, they were silent. Their green feathers matched the green of the leaf canopy, an ideal camouflage. Ramirez did not observe them together with other macaws species.

The mating season of *guyaquilensis* begins with the onset of the rainy season in December. At this time the humidity is at its highest. The nominate form starts to breed about the beginning of January in the Colombian part of its range. In Central America the breeding season begins a few weeks later. There are no further details about breeding habits. It can be assumed, however, that up to three eggs, about 55 x 46 mm. (Schönwetter 1964) are laid, which the female alone incubates. The nestling period of the young probably lasts about one hundred days.

Care and Breeding. The Great Green Macaw has always been extremely rare among bird fanciers. Only occasionally have a few isolated specimens entered Europe along with other macaw species. It can certainly be said that the Great Green Macaw is even more rare than the Hyacinth Macaw (*Anodorhynchus hyacinthinus*), for example, not only in the wild but also in zoos and the aviaries of bird fanciers. It is quite unfortunate that the few animals in captivity are for the most part maintained by fanciers as single birds.

The Great Green Macaw is a bird which forms quite close attachments to people and attracts additional friends because of its great talent for speaking; yet these qualities should not prevent one from buying a mate, to give the birds a chance, with optimal accommodations, to breed. The scarcity of these macaws demands breeding efforts immediately, because importation from their ever-

W.T. Greene, like others since, was puzzled why
Linnaeus chose to give *Ara militaris* "a soldierly
designation."

Honduras
Nicaragua
Costa Rica
Panama

ambigua

Colombia

guyaquilensis

Ecuador

Great Green Macaw
(Ara ambigua)

diminishing natural habitat will be possible only for a short time.

The Tierpark in Berlin, in the German Democratic Republic, reported an authentic successful breeding of the Great Green Macaw. No successful breedings in the Federal Republic are known, but they have taken place in England and the United States. The available information is scant and for the most part gives rise to the suspicion that it may be about breeding the Military Macaw (*Ara militaris*). In the English literature one seldom finds a taxonomic distinction between the Great Green and the Military macaws, so information can quickly become faulty.

M. Reynolds (1977) reports a successful hand-rearing of the Great Green Macaw at Paradise Park in Cornwall. In 1972, a presumed cock was acquired. A good year later, when the bird park came into possession of a hen, this was confirmed, for the two birds accepted one another from the start. Like another macaw pair, the Great Green Macaws were kept at liberty. However, after the macaws in 1974 and 1975 extended their flights farther and farther and had to be retrieved from telephone poles and the highest trees, it was decided to clip some of the flight feathers of their wings. Thus their activities were somewhat limited in the summer of 1976. A short while after the "wing clipping" in April 1976, the female macaw became interested nest boxes and then chose the smallest one. Soon afterward, the female laid two eggs, which she incubated tightly. During the first days of incubation, the male did not bother with the female at all, but a week later he constantly climbed into the nest, which led to altercations, and the result was that the eggs were smashed. There were no more breeding activities in 1976.

A year later the female again took over a small nest box. On May 5, two eggs were discovered. In light of the bad experience of the previous year, these were removed. One egg was placed under a mixed macaw pair, a Scarlet Macaw (*Ara macao*) and a Yellow-collared Macaw (*Ara auricollis*), which were just sitting on eggs. The second egg went into an incubator. A third egg, laid after May 5, was placed under a pair of Scarlet Macaws (*Ara macao*) which were also on eggs. The egg in the incubator developed, but died before hatching. With the mixed macaw pair, a chick from their own eggs

hatched, along with the Great Green Macaw chick. Unfortunately, both chicks lived only three days. Regarding the Scarlet Macaw pair, which had been given the third egg, a chick hatched on June 3, which was assumed to be a Scarlet Macaw. Nothing came of the other eggs, so the hope of rearing a Great Green Macaw had to be laid to rest.

The young bird was reared well by the at-liberty Scarlet Macaw pair. On July 7, it was decided to inspect the nest box, which was done with great caution because the parents were very aggressive. It was found that the chick had a completely different appearance from those reared in previous years. The chick had a round shape, a massive head, and the whole body was covered with thick gray down. A week later the red frontal band became evident, which established positively that the youngster was a Great Green Macaw. In the seventh week the green feathers had broken through, as well as the wing and tail feathers. On August 10, at the age of ten weeks, the youngster was taken from the nest box and hand-reared until it fledged, to prevent it from flying away. The macaw chick very quickly got used to hand-feeding, which was done with a syringe, and it grew splendidly.

Stuttgart's zoo, the Wilhelma, has been able for several years to report hybrid offspring of a male *Ara ambigua* and a female *Ara macao*. The mixed breeding pair was for a long time kept with other macaw species in an indoor flight. Despite the daily stream of visitors, they were not distracted from breeding. In the fall of 1981, when the new outdoor aviary complex for parrots was completed, the other macaws were taken out and put in the new enclosure. The mixed breeding pair were left in the indoor flight in the hope that the hybrid breedings would be even more productive in the future. The offspring of this macaw pair, in the meanwhile, occupy a beautiful outdoor flight at the Wilhelma. Although hybrid breeding is dismissed by taxonomists and breeders, this success is nevertheless remarkable and scientifically valuable. The Wilhelma birds are very attractively colored and full of energy; they are constantly in motion, playing and romping with each other.

It is to be hoped that the few German fanciers possessing Great Green Macaws will join together to make arrangements to attempt to breed this rare species.

1, 2, 3. With the Great Green Macaw *(Ara ambigua),* it is extremely difficult to make subspecific identifications. It is also difficult to determine its relationship with the Military Macaw *(Ara militaris).* **2.** Mutual preening is an important part of the social life of macaws. The Red-and-green Macaw *(Ara chloroptera),* evidently at ease, is enjoying the activity.

1. Red-and-green Macaws *(Ara chloroptera)*. 2. Scarlet Macaws *(Ara macao)*. 3. Red-and-green Macaw. 4. Scarlet Macaws. 5. Head study of a Red-and-green Macaw. 6. Scarlet Macaw. 7. Red-and-green Macaw hen with two chicks.

Red-and-green Macaw
Ara chloroptera
G. R. Gray 1859

Characteristics. Size, about 90 cm. Dark red. Median and greater wing coverts various shades of green. Outer vanes of greater wing coverts blue. Primaries and secondaries blue. Outer vanes of primaries dark blue. Underside of wings dark brownish red. Rump and upper tail coverts light blue. Tail feathers dark red, becoming blue at the tip. Outer vanes of outer tail feathers blue. Bare facial area whitish, traversed with lines of red feathers. Upper mandible horn color, dark gray on the sides toward the base. Lower mandible blackish gray. Iris yellow. Toes dark gray brown. Female like the male, but somewhat more slender in body. Young birds like adults, but iris brownish.

Range. South and east of the Canal Zone in Panama to the Golfo de Cupica in western Colombia. Northern Colombia along the Caribbean coast to northwestern Venezuela. Eastern Colombia along the Andes southward through eastern Peru, northern and eastern Bolivia, Paraguay, and Formosa in northern Argentina to Paraná in Brazil. From Venezuela eastward through the Guianas to eastern Maranhão and from there southward to Paraná (Brazil).

Way of Life. The Red-and-green Macaw is, next to the Hyacinth Macaw (*Anodorhynchus hyacinthinus*), the largest parrot. Compared to the Hyacinth Macaw, it is about 10 cm. less in body size, but its powerful build, massive head, and large, powerful beak leave a formidable impression.

The Red-and-green Macaw is found in much the same area as its close relative, the Scarlet Macaw (*Ara macao*). The Red-and-green Macaw is a bird of the virgin tropical lowland forests and edges and mainly occupies biotopes up to an altitude of 450 m. Sporadically the macaws are found at heights to 1400 m. where they inhabit subtropical-zone or dry forests. The Red-and-green Macaws do not form large flocks, but mostly live in pairs, families, or small groups. More than six seldom forage together.

In the last century Red-and-green Macaws still occupied the lowlands west of the Canal Zone in Panama; today they are no longer found in these areas. The present-day range of these macaws ends in the eastern part of the Cordillera de San Blas in Panama. The small mountain peaks in the eastern part of Panama, not very high, act as a boundary to the spacious lowlands of Darién and are home to the macaws, especially in the backcountry of the Carribbean coast. Hot and humid tropical forests, mangrove swamps, and savannas characterize the sparsely inhabited natural landscape here, as well as in northern Colombia. In Colombia the macaws occur in the valleys of the Atrato and the Magdalena and their tributaries, with their virgin tropical forests; the lower slopes of the Sierra Nevada de Santa Marta; and west and east of the Sierra de Perijá, which to the east slopes toward the Lago de Maracaibo in Venezuela. The Red-and-green Macaw is not found north of the Orinoco in Venezuela, from Portuguesa to Monagas. It occurs locally in areas south of the Orinoco and its tributaries and in the Orinoco Delta.

In Guyana, Suriname, and French Guiana, the animals are found in the interior, behind the coastal strip, about 30 km. wide and studded with mangroves. In some places in the highland rain shadow, the thinly-settled rainforests are broken up by hilly savannas. These macaws do not appear to be common in the Guianas; the Scarlet Macaw is far more numerous. In Brazil the Red-and-green Macaw is abandoning more and more the Atlantic coastal forests and retreating into the interior to live in the great riverine areas with their virgin forests. In some areas the Red-and-green Macaws are the most numerous macaws. P. Roth (pers. comm.) reports that in northernmost Mato Grosso the Red-and-green Macaw is found more often in the dry season than in the rainy season. It eats relatively large fruits, especially hard-shelled ones, such as uxí (*Endopleura uchi*), jatobá (*Hymenala* sp.), or the unripe fruits of *Bertholletia excelsa*.

In eastern Colombia, eastern Peru, and eastern Bolivia the macaws occur only locally, even where vast virgin-forest tracts and the virgin forest along rivers are readily available to them. In Paraguay the Red-and-green Macaw is restricted largely to the marsh region. Probably only seasonal wandering takes them into Chaco and Formosa (Argentina).

The breeding season coincides with that of other macaw species occurring in the same area. Thus,

Panama

Venezuela

Guyana

Suriname

French Guiana

Colombia

Ecuador

Peru

Brazil

Bolivia

Paraguay

Argentina

Red-and-green Macaw
(Ara chloroptera)

1, 2. Red-fronted Macaw *(Ara rubrogenys).* When frightened, newly imported parrots often retreat as far as possible from the perceived threat, and hang in a cluster. 3. Red-and-green Macaw *(Ara chloroptera).* These 4-week-old chicks were bred by G. Wilking.

Successful captive breedings of the Red-and-green Macaw *(Ara chloroptera)* have been numerous, both in zoos and bird parks and in the hands of private aviculturists.

breeding activities begin in November and December in the south and in February and March in the north. Hollow tree trunks or holes in damaged palms very high above the ground serve as nesting places. Red-and-green Macaws usually prefer to remain in the tops of trees and palms. They descend to the ground only to ingest mineral-rich earth. As many as three eggs, about 50 x 35 mm. in size, are incubated by the female for about twenty-eight days. Rearing the young, which lasts some ninety to one hundred days, is carried out by both parents. After leaving the nest, the macaw chicks remain with the parents for a long time.

Care and Breeding. The Red-and-green Macaw, along with the Blue-and-yellow Macaw (*Ara ararauna*) and the Scarlet Macaw (*Ara macao*), is one of the most frequently imported macaws. Every zoological garden and bird park exhibits these colorful macaws in its enclosures. They are for the most part housed with other macaw species, and this frequently results in hybrid offspring.

The Red-and-green Macaw is by nature a delightful house pet that quickly becomes tame and also learns to say a few words. Red-and-green Macaws may be highly recommended as pets, since they become closely attached to their owners. The author once kept a tame Red-and-green Macaw in an aviary with Blue-and-yellow Macaws, Scarlet Macaws, and a Great Green Macaw (*Ara ambigua*). The Red-and-green Macaw was the calming element in the little group. As soon as an altercation arose between the other aviary inhabitants over a piece of apple or a better perch, it interposed itself as a peacemaker and each time succeeded in bringing the "fighting cocks" to their senses. It allowed itself to be scratched on the head, belly, and under the wings with the greatest delight. If the scratching ever got to be too much, and this was very seldom, it would carefully take one's finger in its massive beak and gingerly push the hand aside.

The world's first successful breeding of the Red-and-green Macaw probably occurred in England in 1962. The breeding pair had tried in vain for a successful breeding in 1960 and 1961, and in 1962 two young were reared from a clutch of three eggs. The first egg was laid in April, but this embryo died. The other eggs must have been laid in June, because in July the peeping of two birds could be heard. The adults were very quiet during the breeding season; but they defended their breeding area, the aviary and the nest box, with extreme aggressiveness, so that inspection of the nest box was not possible. It is worth noting that the female stayed in the nest box constantly for the first five weeks and brooded the chicks. When the young birds were 103 days old, they left the nest. This successful breeding pair is reported to have raised twenty-eight young birds in a period of fifteen years.

The first successful rearing of purebred Red-and-green Macaws in Germany occurred in 1970 at the Hannover zoo. In 1972, in the aviaries of a Texas bird fancier, three chicks hatched, according to laying interval, after twenty-seven days. After four days, the youngest chick was placed under a breeding pair of Scarlet Macaws (*Ara macao*), because it was no longer being fed by its parents. Three weeks later it was taken for hand-rearing. The other two chicks were cared for by the parents without difficulties.

The German parrot fancier G. Wilking was able to report a successful breeding of Red-and-green Macaws in 1980. He had owned a female since 1975, and he bought a male in late May 1980. Both hand-tame birds settled into an indoor flight with dimensions of 1.5 x 2.4 x 2.3 m. The nest box installed in the flight had an area 55 x 70 cm. and a height of 1 m. The entrance hole bored in the upper third of the nest box had a diameter of 22 cm. The floor of the nest box was covered with 10 cm. of a mixture of sawdust and peat.

Both macaws accepted one another from the start. After only a few days they began to investigate the hanging nest box. The first attempts at treading took place after the birds had been together for three weeks. Copulations occurred on June 16, 22, and 26 and always took place in the afternoon between four and five p.m. The first egg was laid on June 29, the second three days later, on July 2. On July 5, the eggs were candled, and it looked as if only one was fertile. An inspection on July 18 revealed a third egg in the nest box. All of the eggs were fertile; however, the first egg laid had a crack about 3 cm. long. A thin protective layer of instant glue was put over the crack. After twenty-eight days of incubation, on July 26, a chick hatched from the patched egg. Two days later a chick emerged from the second egg. Unfortunately, the third egg was crushed before hatching. The size of the gleaming white eggs was 46.0 x 34.8 mm. The female incubated alone, but the male spent the nights in the nest box.

Both youngsters grew well. After eight days the first down feathers appeared. At fifteen days their eyes opened. In their third week the first feather sheaths emerged, and the upper and lower mandibles took on a slightly darker color on the edges at the base. One week later, the sheaths of the wing and tail feathers opened. After five weeks, the red feathers on the head were evident, the beak continued to color up, and the wing and tail feathers were 2–3 cm. long. The size and feathering of the youngsters now increased very rapidly. On October 23, both little macaws were fully feathered, and in their thirteenth week they left the nest box.

The food offered during the rearing period was as follows: sunflower seed (dry and sprouted), fresh corn, different kinds of nuts, fruit of every kind, a mixed-fruit pap (Milupa) mixed with curd cheese, soaked zwieback, finely chopped egg, and a multivitamin powder.

In the Wuppertal zoological garden three Red-and-green Macaws were reared in 1975 and 1976. Afterward, one of the breeding pair escaped. Far more successful was their hybrid breeding between a Blue-and-yellow Macaw and a Red-and-green Macaw. Dr. Schürer told the author that by 1980 they had raised forty chicks. In 1960, the large parrots at the Wuppertal Zoo had new accommodations once the outdoor parrot aviaries were set up. A year later it was noticed that a Blue-and-yellow Macaw (Ara ararauna) and a Red-and-Green Macaw had developed a friendship and were defending their perches and feeding places against the other inhabitants of the flight. The animals sat together all the time and preened one another. In 1962 the first copulation occurred; at the same time they became aggressive toward the other occupants. When egg laying began, they were immediately put into the winter quarters. Although a suitable nest box was at their disposal here, the new accommodations were not accepted by the animals.

The housing next chosen for the two macaws probably did not suit their tastes either, although eggs were laid on July 4, 7, and 10, 1963. The eggs were laid on the ground and remained there

unnoticed. Following this, the macaw pair were returned to the outdoor flight. The eggs laid early in July were immediately placed in an incubator with a temperature of 37.8 C. and 65% humidity. Three times daily the eggs were aired for a period of ten minutes and turned. After an incubation period of twenty-six days (the natural incubation period is twenty-eight days), the chick in the first egg laid pipped. At this time, humidity was raised to 87% by means of a basin of water and wet towels. Fifty hours later, after the chick had stopped pipping and the peeping was slowly quieting, hatching assistance was given, and the baby bird was freed from the shell. The egg laid on July 7 was pipped on the morning of August 1. A few hours later, the chick hatched. The youngster in the egg laid on July 10 started pipping on August 3 and was free twenty-four hours later. The artificial incubation lasted exactly twenty-five days, though with the first egg laid it was twenty-six days. It is significant that the first egg was slightly overcooled when it was put into the incubator; also, at the time of hatching, humidity was not sufficiently high, causing the hatching process to take more than fifty hours. The average weight of the eggs was 30 g., and the hatching weight of the chicks was between 25 and 26 g.

Information from the San Diego Zoo indicated that the ideal temperature for rearing is between 32 and 35 C. In order to ensure a uniform temperature, the chicks were put into a plastic basket, which permitted a certain amount of air circulation in the brooder. The temperature set was 33.5 C. with 80% humidity. This temperature was the most favorable for the digestive process, as indigestion occurred with the slightest changes in temperature. Between 6 a.m. and 10 p.m. they were fed six times, with an eyedropper. The rearing mixture consisted of a half cup of shredded wheat, two egg yolks, and two tablespoons of powdered milk. This was mixed together, thinned with water to a soupy consistency, and cooked over low heat until it became firm. In addition, curd cheese and bananas were added, so that the final mixture consisted of one part curd cheese, one part bananas, and six parts of the cooked mixture. Half-ripe milky corn and sprouted seeds were also offered. Small amounts of oil seeds were digested easily; but when larger amounts were given, digestive disturbances

1. Hand-tame Scarlet Macaw *(Ara macao)*. **2.** Blue-and-yellow Macaw *(Ara ararauna)*. **3.** On exhibit at Walsrode bird park, the Red-fronted Macaw *(Ara rubrogenys)* has the companionship of a Red-fronted Conure *(Aratinga wagleri)*. **4.** Hybrids of *Ara ararauna* x *chloroptera* bred in the Wuppertal zoo. **5.** The parents of this 15-week-old hybrid were a Scarlet Macaw and a Red-and-green Macaw.

1, 2. Scarlet Macaws kept at liberty. 3. Corn, especially at the half-ripe stage, is relished by macaws. This Red-and-green Macaw *(Ara chloroptera)* holds the ear of corn without difficulty and brings it to its beak with its prehensile toes. 4. A Red-and-green Macaw searching for a nest site. 5. The geographic race *cumanensis* of the Red-shouldered Macaw *(Diopsittaca nobilis)* is distinguished from the nominate form by the light color of the upper mandible; also, this subspecies is noticeably larger. 6. A breeding pair of Red-shouldered Macaws *(Diopsittaca nobilis nobilis)* with their chick sitting on the left. The difference in color between youngsters and adult birds is also noteworthy.

followed. In addition, multivitamins (T-Vitamin-Götsch®, Polyvital®, Sanostol®, and Multimulsin®) were alternated, and now and then some Rovendal® was administered. Since grated cuttlebone did not supply enough calcium, only with doses of Calcipot® did the bones of the chicks develop satisfactorily.

Unfortunately, the first chick to hatch died, but both of the others grew quite well, considering the circumstances. Between the sixtieth and seventieth days of life, at a weight of 375 g., they developed a thick down and the sheaths of the wing and tail feathers broke through. Rapid growth of feathers continued until the ninetieth day. On October 24, at the age of ten weeks, the first wing flapping was seen. On December 22 and 25, the youngsters flew for the first time.

Although crossbreeding is deplored by fanciers and specialists, and even though the Wuppertal zoo does not support such efforts, this successful hand-rearing of hybrid macaws must be regarded as particularly remarkable. In keeping parrots, all breeding activity that promises success, regardless of whether it is purebred or "only" related species, should be encouraged with every available means of assistance.

From 1964 on, the macaw pair (a male Blue-and-yellow Macaw and a female Red-and-green Macaw) had their own place, with a nest box at their disposal, and each year they regularly reared chicks to independence. Egg laying proceeded at intervals of two to three days. Incubation is always done by the hen, although the cock often climbs into the nest box. Feeding the chicks is handled by both parents. Since macaws incubate from the first day of egg laying and chicks hatch in the order of laying, it is not at all unusual that the youngest chick may be shoved aside by the larger ones at feeding time and therefore starve. As mentioned previously, at the Wuppertal zoo between 1963 and 1980, forty chicks were reared by the productive breeding pair. There has not been any report of a successful breeding by the F₁ generation; however, fertile eggs have already been laid.

It is hoped that in the future more fanciers will devote themselves to the Red-and-green Macaw and will try to bring about successful breedings of these animals. In any case, they are highly recommended and during the breeding season they are very quiet.

Scarlet Macaw
Ara macao
(Linnaeus 1758)

Characteristics. Size, about 85 cm. Brilliant red. Wings and wing coverts blue. Greater wing coverts and shoulder coverts yellow, part with blue and green tips. Primaries and secondaries blue. Underside of wings red. Lower back, rump, and upper and under tail coverts light blue. Tail red, blue toward the tip. Iris yellow. Bare eye-cheek area completely unfeathered, whitish, sometimes flesh color. Upper mandible horn color, with a black triangle at the base. Lower mandible black. Toes gray brown. Female colored like the male; beak somewhat smaller; forehead often somewhat flatter. Young birds colored like adults; somewhat more slender; iris brown; toes brown.

Range. From southern Tamaulipas along the Caribbean coast through Vera Cruz and Tabasco to southern Campeche and Oaxaca and Chiapas (Mexico); through Belize and Guatemala southward along the Andes to Santa Cruz in Bolivia and northern Mato Grosso in Brazil, eastward to Pará in Brazil.

Way of Life. In the northernmost part of its range, Vera Cruz and Oaxaca in Mexico, the Scarlet Macaw is decreasing in numbers very sharply. In some localities where the birds were present in great numbers years ago they have already died out; in other areas only small numbers are found locally. In southern Tamaulipas (Mexico), the macaws occur only locally and occasionally. Scarlet Macaws are lowland birds that are found at altitudes of 900 m. at most. In Guatemala the macaws occur mainly in western Petén, especially along the river Usumacinta, which separates Mexico and Guatemala, as well as along a few of its tributaries. The birds are extremely rare on the narrow Pacific coastal strip. In Belize (formerly British Honduras) Scarlet Macaws are found in the coastal backcountry, which in the north is as wide as 75

Scarlet Macaw *(Ara macao)*

Dr. Greene begins his chapter on the "Red and Blue Macaw" *(Ara macao)* thus: "This grand bird is, without a doubt, king of all the Macaws. . . ."

km. because of alluvial deposits. Likewise, the birds populate the river courses, which are bordered by great swamp forests. The annual rainfall—there are two not very pronounced rainy seasons—amounts to 1500 mm. in the north and 3000 mm. in the humid south.

In the most densely populated country of Central America, El Salvador, occurrence of this macaw is limited to the southeastern, almost uninhabited coastal section and the forest area around the Lago de Olomega. The rainy and dry seasons are very distinct in El Salvador, unlike Belize. The rainy season, in which 96% of the rain falls, lasts from May to October. In populated areas the original vegetation, cleared by burning, is no longer extant; it remains only in the inaccessible southern coastal regions and in riverine and highland areas. The civil-warlike conditions that persist even now affect nature as well as the populace. The present food shortage compels people to shoot wild animals to provide themselves with the barest necessities.

In Honduras, Scarlet Macaws inhabit the precipitation-poor Pacific coastal areas. In the hilly highlands of northeastern and eastern Honduras, traversed by many rivers, this macaw occurs in riverine forests up to an altitude of 1100 m. In Nicaragua, the birds can be found more on the Pacific coast than on the Caribbean. The situation is the same in Costa Rica: here Scarlet Macaws are found more often in the Pacific coastal backcountry; though they cross the narrow country to the Caribbean coast, they are far more scarce there.

In Panama, as in the countries just mentioned, a sharp decline in the number of macaws is evident; in the Canal Zone the birds are already completely gone. The Serranía de Tabasara, a mountain chain in western Panama, is a climatic barrier, just like the Cordillera de Talamanca in Costa Rica. The Pacific region has a tropical, variably humid climate with savannas in the coastal area. The Caribbean side, which is almost uninhabited, is always moist and therefore covered with tropical rainforest that extends to the coast. The locality favored by the Scarlet Macaws is limited to part of the Azuero Peninsula and the island of Coiba. These macaws have also been recorded on the islands Canal de Afuera and Rancheria in recent years. From the Isla Rancheria it has been reported that the macaws fly back and forth between the island and the mainland.

In the vicinity of the town of Rio de Jesus, the author several times saw small groups of eight to twelve birds in flight. Presumed pairs would fly very close together, almost touching each other. In the oblique rays of the evening sun the red feathers glowed especially brightly. It is a glorious sight to observe these great parrots in flight, for only then does the coloration of the flight feathers come to the fore.

The Central American part of their range ends at the Isthmus of Panama; it resumes on the South American continent at the mouth of the Atrato on the Golfo de Urabá in Colombia. Scarlet Macaws are still relatively common in the valley of the Rio Magdalena in northwestern Colombia; here the populace likes to keep them as cage birds. The range continues southward along the eastern side of the Andes to Santa Cruz in Bolivia. The habitat preferred here is mainly the dry forest during the rainy season; moist rainforests are merely passed over in flight. In Venezuela, Guyana, Suriname, French Guiana, and Brazil the macaws likewise prefer to dwell in the dry forests and savannas, where they are found at heights up to about 1000 m. They are more common during the rainy season. Even here the areas inhabited by people are to a great extent avoided. It is terribly difficult to track down the shy birds; as a result of being hunted for centuries, they maintain a very great fleeing distance from man. In Trinidad, the macaws were observed only in 1934 and 1943 (ffrench 1976). Two Scarlet Macaws were seen in October 1934 in the Nariva Swamp, a mangrove-swamp area in the eastern part of the island; in May 1943, five birds stopped in the vicinity of the city Arima (Waller Field) in the hilly interior.

Scarlet Macaws, except during the breeding season, live in small family units and form flocks of as many as thirty birds. Like most macaw species, Scarlet Macaws also have a regular, fixed daily routine. For long periods certain trees are preferred as so-called sleeping trees, which they fly to regularly in the late afternoon hours and occupy for the night. Pairs, for the most part, sit close together in order to engage in a great deal of mutual preening before the approach of darkness. Often, with loud shrieks, there are fights over the best sleeping places; thus birds can be detected at great distances. Apparently Scarlet Macaws occasionally use tree cavities for sleeping even outside the breeding season. P. Roth (on July 16, 1978, at 6:20 p.m.) observed that a pair of Scarlet Macaws flew to a very tall tree and immediately sought out a hole located about 25 m. above the ground in which to spend the night.

After sunrise – in the tropics, dawn is very short – the small band then flies off in search of food. Distances of from twenty to thirty km. are often traversed in order to reach the fruit-bearing food trees. Several species of palm fruits, figs, mangos, etc., serve as food for the macaws. It is doubtful that the macaws also come down to the ground to eat, although Scarlet Macaws can be seen on the sloping banks where they eat the salt-bearing clay. At such "mineral sources" a variety of macaw species often congregate, presenting the most colorful picture one could ever imagine.

Scarlet Macaws probably also eat animal food (P. Roth). In November 1978, a pair of *Ara macao* were observed regularly visiting a tree cavity about 30 m. high. An inspection of the presumed nest hole yielded neither eggs nor young. In the rotting wood at the bottom of the cavity there were a great number of beetle larvae of the superfamily *Lamellicornia*, 10 cm. long. The suspicion arises that the macaws sought out the cavity to gather the larvae. Since the breeding season was in full progress at this time, it can be surmised that they were collecting animal protein as supplementary food for their offspring.

During the breeding season, pairs separate from the flock in order to pursue breeding activities. One assumes that the macaws use their own nesting cavities every year, as long as these are usable. Because of the size of the birds, only spacious holes are possible nesting places, and the supply of these cannot be all that large. Most of the nesting places available are in dead palms. Palms, with their smooth, tall trunks, offer the surest protection from nest robbers. On the other hand, cavities in large trees and holes in the earth of sloping banks are also used by the animals. The breeding season starts in December, or even November, in the southern part of the range. In the most northern part, in Mexico, the breeding season does not begin until later, about March or April.

As a rule, two to four eggs are laid, somewhat smaller in size than chicken eggs: 47.0 x 33.9 mm.,

elliptical (Schönwetter 1964). The egg-laying interval varies from three to five days. Since incubation by the female begins on the first day of egg laying, the youngsters hatch at intervals after twenty-five or twenty-six days. It is believed that the male stays in the vicinity of the nest hole and keeps watch. No information is available about the course of incubation and rearing the young in the wild. It is known that the young are fully able to fly when they leave the nest and that for several weeks they will be guided by the parents.

Care and Breeding. Next to the Blue-and-yellow Macaw (*Ara ararauna*) and the Red-and-green Macaw (*Ara chloroptera*), the Scarlet Macaw is the best known and the most widely kept by fanciers. Brought to Spain on the riches-laden ships of the first Spaniards to visit Central America in the fifteenth and sixteenth centuries, the splendidly colored birds from there found their way to all European countries.

Kept singly, the Scarlet Macaw is a bird that becomes tame very quickly and even learns to say a few words. As a bird of the tropical lowlands, one should always take care that accommodations are appropriate to such a species; thus the Scarlet Macaw should not be kept at temperatures lower than 18 C. Of course, the birds can endure temperatures far lower, but they will never feel comfortable in them.

The first successful breedings of the Scarlet Macaw are said to have occurred for an American, Chamness, in 1916. In subsequent years, his Scarlet Macaw pair repeatedly raised young, as many as three chicks per breeding. In England the first successful breeding took place in 1934.

In Germany the first pure breeding of Scarlet Macaws was achieved in 1980 by K. and R. Fuhs, brother and sister. In the autumn of 1977, the Fuhses acquired two Scarlet Macaws which were on exhibit at a bird show. By chance, the two birds were staged nearby during the show and took a liking to each other. For a year, the birds were kept in the living room, and with constant human contact they soon became very tame. The somewhat smaller bird became especially confiding and allowed its entire body to be stroked with the fingers.

The macaws were next housed in an indoor flight

in a conservatory. The flight itself measured 150 x 250 x 250 cm. Two other indoor flights housed pairs of Little Corellas (*Cacatua sanguinea*) and Salmon-crested Cockatoos (*Cacatua moluccensis*). When the macaws showed increasing interest in each other and the large bird was feeding the smaller, a nest box of 55 x 55 x 110 cm. was installed in the flight. A short time later, the smaller macaw investigated the box in detail. After December 29, 1979, even the "big guy" showed an interest in the nest box; from this it was presumed that the smaller macaw was the hen and the larger was the cock. Thereafter, the female was really aggressive and defended the nest box, which she left only twice a day. On February 29, 1980, the first egg, somewhat smaller than a hen's egg, was found; a second was laid four days later. Thirty-two days after the second egg was laid, the eggs were removed because both were infertile. On April 12, 1980, attempts at treading were seen for the first time, and on April 25 and 29, 1980, egg laying again occurred.

After an incubation period of exactly twenty-five days, on May 19, 1980, the first chick hatched. The begging cries of the baby bird became softer and softer, and on May 22 the chick was dead. The second chick emerged four and a half days after the first, on May 23, 1980. The macaws were now watched very closely. Special attention was paid to the young bird, in order to be able to intervene immediately at the first sign of neglect by the adults and to help the little one by rearing it by hand. Everything went off perfectly, however, and intervention was unnecessary.

Since the hen stayed in the nest box constantly until the youngster was sixty days old, the cock alone ate the food offered, but without touching the supplementary food, which consisted of Milupa® infant diet, dog chow (Biohundeflocken®), zwieback, and rearing food. Only sunflower seed, cembra-pine nuts, peanuts, carrots, grapes, and oranges were eaten. The various kinds of food were eaten in a noteworthy pattern, alternating between a few seeds or nuts and pieces of fruit, so that food intake repeatedly varied between "hard" and "soft" foods.

The youngster was covered with yellow down feathers by the third day. On the seventeenth day, the first feather sheaths had already appeared, and body size had increased threefold. After forty-two days, the first colored feathers were recognizable on the back, head, and wings. The lower mandible, as well as the triangular spot on the base of the upper mandible, which are dark in fledged Scarlet Macaws, on the twenty-fifth day began gradually to change from horn color to black. The feathering increased rapidly from this point on. By the forty-ninth day, the colored wing feathers were well grown out, and the body and tail feathering increased apace. The red feathers on the back, breast, and belly developed somewhat more slowly and until the seventieth day seemed very downy. By day 105 the youngster was fully feathered and distinguishable from the parents only by its slightly smaller body size. The hen remained in the nest box until the chick was sixty days old, during which she was fed by the cock; thereafter she got her own food. After the ninetieth day the adult birds ate noticeably less food; apparently, from this time on, the young bird no longer needed the quantity of food hitherto delivered. At this young age the young Scarlet Macaw showed an interest in its environment; it frequently stuck its body halfway out of the nest hole and tested the surroundings nearby with its beak. At the age of 105 days the youngster left the nest for good.

The Fuhses attributed the successful breeding of Scarlet Macaws to the fact that both adult birds were hand-tame and that they knew their owners very well. During the course of breeding the birds were often disturbed, because the cockatoo pair also housed in the conservatory frequently screamed incredibly loudly. In order to keep the neighborhood from being further annoyed by the birds' alarm calls, it was necessary to enter the flight constantly to calm them, with the result that the macaws were disturbed very often. The author too believes that the breeding was brought to a successful conclusion only because the breeding pair was so confiding toward the owners.

A successful breeding of Scarlet Macaws very worth mentioning took place at the Jerome Buteyn Bird Ranch in San Luis Rey, California. A very large aviary held other macaws along with the Scarlet Macaws. After it was noticed that the Scarlet Macaws showed an inclination to breed, the other birds were taken out, with great difficulty. Of the many nest boxes offered, the one chosen by the

Scarlet Macaw pair stood directly on the floor of the aviary. The dimensions of this box were considerable—an area of 120 x 120 cm. and a height of about 60 cm.—but it suited the wishes of the macaws. The nest depression was made by the animals themselves. Eight days after the removal of the other occupants, the first egg lay in the nest, and the female immediately started incubation. Altogether the female laid three eggs. Inspection undertaken later revealed three youngsters. Two weeks later it was confirmed that all three youngsters were still alive and doing well. The three chicks were reared successfully by the adults. For food the macaws were offered various seeds, bread, tomatoes, and fruit, as well as calcium.

The remarkable thing about this breeding is that *three* young birds were reared. It is well known that macaws often kill the second or third chick shortly after hatching and rear only one, or sometimes two. Probably killing the young is natural behavior, because it is hardly conceivable that in the wild the macaws can provide three or more young birds with food; the chicks consume an incredibly large amount, and the adults are not in a position to provide an unlimited quantity. One should also realize that in the tropics dawn and dusk are short, and the day there is only twelve to thirteen hours long.

Hybrid breedings with other large macaw species have been reported several times. Such breeding successes have been achieved principally in zoological gardens, because here the various macaw species often are represented by single specimens. These hybrid breedings in the zoos often took place under the most unfavorable conditions imaginable; but nevertheless, breeding has occurred between the Scarlet Macaw and the Red-and-green Macaw (*Ara chloroptera*), the Great Green Macaw (*Ara ambigua*), the Military Macaw (*Ara militaris*), and the Blue-and-yellow Macaw (*Ara ararauna*). The hybrids resulting from such breedings often display truly attractive colors in parts of their plumage. The Wilhelma, the zoo in Stuttgart, in one aviary exhibits several Great Green x Scarlet hybrids which are mainly green with the entire head red to yellow. The cheeks have thin lines of feathers, and the beak is completely black; these features make it unequivocally clear that the Great Green Macaw is the father.

Genus *DIOPSITTACA* Ridgway 1912

The genus *Diopsittaca* was recently erected. Until a short time ago, the one species contained in it was listed with the "true" macaws. The distinctive characteristic of the genus is the same as that of *Ara*; however, the bare facial area is present only around the eyes and in the loral area. One conspicuous characteristic is the small size, at most 30 cm. No visible sexual characteristics separate males and females. Young birds are distinguishable from adults by color. The genus *Diopsittaca* can be regarded as an intermediate genus between *Ara* and the former genus *Aratinga* ("wedge-tailed parakeets").

Red-shouldered Macaw *Diopsittaca nobilis* (Linnaeus 1758)

Three subspecies:

1. *Diopsittaca nobilis nobilis* (Linnaeus)

Characteristics. Size, about 30 cm. Green. Sides of belly more yellow green. Forehead and forecrown green blue. Bend of wing, under wing coverts, and carpal edge red. Outer vanes of outer secondaries blue. Underside of wings yellow green. Tail green. Underside of tail yellow green. Small bare facial area, extending from around the eyes to the lores and base of the upper mandible, white. Iris orange brown. Beak grayish black. Toes dark gray. Female like the male; head somewhat more slender. Young birds like adults, but forehead and forecrown green; bend of wing, carpal edge, and lower wing coverts show little red.

Range. Eastern Venezuela, the Guianas, and north of the Amazon in northeastern Roraima, northern Pará, and Amapá in Brazil.

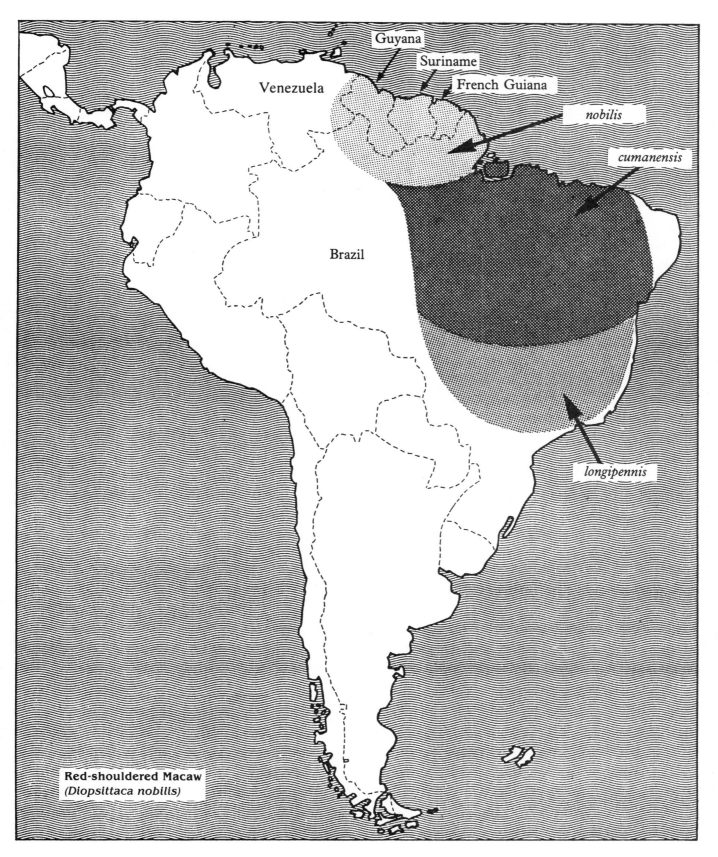

Guyana

Suriname

French Guiana

Venezuela

nobilis

cumanensis

Brazil

longipennis

Red-shouldered Macaw
(Diopsittaca nobilis)

2. *Diopsittaca nobilis cumanensis* (Lichtenstein)

Characteristics. Like the nominate subspecies, but noticeably larger; upper mandible horn color with a gray tip; lower mandible dark gray.

Range. Brazil south of the Amazon in Pará, Maranhão, Piauí, western Pernambuco, Bahia, and northern Goiás.

3. *Diopsittaca nobilis longipennis* Neumann

Characteristics. Like *cumanensis*, but larger.

Range. Brazil: eastern Mato Grosso, southern Goiás, Minas Gerais, western Espírito Santo, and northern São Paulo.

Way of Life. All three geographical races of the Red-shouldered Macaw, the smallest member in all four genera of macaws, are birds of the tropical zone. The animals inhabit the lowlands and are rarely found at altitudes over 400 m. Outside the breeding season, the macaws roam about their range in large groups; in this they differ markedly from related genera, the species of which forage only in pairs, in family groups, or in small flocks. This behavior shows the close relationship of the genus *Diopsittaca* to the species of the *Aratinga* group, which sometimes move about in very large flocks.

The range of the Red-shouldered Macaw in eastern Venezuela is limited to an area south of the Orinoco Delta in southern Amacuro and eastern Bolivar, where only limited local occurrence has been confirmed. In the Guianas the Red-shouldered Macaw is very well represented, living mainly in the tropical coastal backcountry. Open palm forests are a favored habitat. The birds even enter the outskirts of cities.

The author was able to observe large flocks of these macaws at the outer edges of Georgetown and New Amsterdam (Guyana). He also noticed that some White-eyed Conures (*Psittacara*, formerly *Aratinga, leucophthalmus leucophthalmus*) mingled with the macaw flocks. The macaws were distinguishable from the conures only by the light bare cheek patches and the dark beak. On the other

hand, there were no characteristics of shape or action in flight which would have made distinction possible. The undersides of the wing in both species are almost the same color, and rapid flight with jerky wing beats is typical of both species. It is hard to believe the amount of noise these macaws make while flying; with a favorable wind, a flock can be heard a good kilometer away. The author, during his stay in Georgetown, was regularly awakened in the morning by the cries of Red-shouldered Macaws and Orange-winged Amazons (*Amazona amazonica amazonica*).

North of the Amazon in Brazil, the birds occupy landscapes like those in the northern part of their range. Likewise, with the subspecies *cumanensis* and *longipennis* there doesn't seem to be any essential difference in the biotopes used; i.e., these macaws also prefer open landscapes.

A permanent pair bond such as we have seen in the larger macaws of related genera doesn't seem to occur in the Red-shouldered Macaw. Of course, this particular topic is not being studied, so all observations, by breeders as well, are of especial interest.

At the beginning of the breeding season the Red-shouldered Macaws separate from the flock. In the north the breeding season starts sometime in March; in the southernmost part of the range it begins in November or December. Up to five eggs are laid, about 31 x 25 mm. in size. They are incubated for about twenty-four days (very different data have been advanced about the incubation period, varying from twenty-four to twenty-eight days). It is conceivable that the males participate in incubating the eggs; at least, they often stay with the females in the nest holes at this time. After a nestling period of some sixty days, the fledged youngsters leave the nest.

Richard ffrench (1976) reports that in October 1934, two Red-shouldered Macaws were seen in the Nariva Swamp (eastern Trinidad). In 1968 a single bird was observed at Pointe-à-Pierre (western Trinidad). It is conceivable that the single animal was an escaped cage bird (today gigantic petroleum depots are located near Pointe-à-Pierre). Of course, it doesn't seem at all strange that in previous years Red-shouldered Macaws occurred in Trinidad, since the delta at the mouth of the Orinoco, where the macaws are indigenous, lies directly opposite the southern coast of Trinidad. Moreover, a skin of this macaw in the British Museum at Tring, which was received from the London Zoo, is said to have come from Trinidad.

Care and Breeding. Red-shouldered Macaws are very seldom imported. Since Brazil has enacted an absolute ban on the export of native animal species, only the nominate form, *Diopsittaca nobilis*, is available to fanciers. Because of its small size and "unmacawlike" feather coloration, Red-shouldered Macaws often are not even recognized as macaws. An animal dealer in the Rhineland once offered the author Red-shouldered Macaws as "Bare-cheeked Parakeets." The salesman claimed the birds came from a German breeder and were native to Chile. Another dealer offered Red-shouldered Macaws as young "Red-masked Conures". If a bird fancier wishes to buy a bird from an advertisement, he should first telephone the seller to get information about the appearance of the bird, in order to guarantee that they are really dealing with the species advertised.

Housing is not so great a problem with Red-shouldered Macaws as it is with the larger macaws. A wide choice of cages and indoor flights is available commercially, to provide a satisfactory solution for every pocketbook. Singly kept Red-shouldered Macaws become tame quickly. The author has seen birds which allowed themselves to be laid on their backs by their owners and tickled on their bellies. At the same time, the birds are very adept at talking; in this respect they are far superior to the large macaw species. The rendering of the words they have learned is not as clear as with the Grey Parrot (*Psittacus erithacus*); however, some can acquire vocabularies as large as many a Grey.

The first successful breeding occurred in 1939 in the United States. Here three youngsters, probably from the race *D. n. cumanensis*, were reared by hand. The macaws kept by the English fancier E. N. T. Vane were very productive. In 1949, the breeding female of the subspecies *D. n. cumanensis* laid eggs on June 10, 12, 16, and 18, and incubated from the first day of egg laying. After an incubation period of twenty-five days, the chicks hatched on July 5, 7, 9, and 12. On September 3, the eldest youngster left the nest, and the others had followed by September 9. The nestling period lasted some

sixty days. The successful breeding pair thereafter reared youngsters regularly. In 1956, the thirtieth young bird left the nest.

In 1963, the first successful German breeding (probably) of a Red-shouldered Macaw took place in the Kleinzoo in Hof. The breeding was reported as the rearing of a Chestnut-fronted Macaw (*Ara severa*), but surely there was some confusion here. In 1960, the successful breeding pair was acquired and housed in an outdoor flight with dimensions 3.0 x 3.0 x 2.5 m., with an attached shelter room 3.0 x 2.0 x 1.3 m. In the spring of 1961, the birds showed interest in a hanging nest box measuring 30 x 30 x 70 cm.; they now defended their nesting area, so that doves also housed in the aviary had to be removed. After this, only one bird could be seen in the aviary, as the second stayed in the nest constantly. Inspection revealed three small, white, almost roundish eggs. The birds resented inspection of the nest so much they they did not return.

In 1962, the macaws were again ready to breed, so there was another attempt. The installed nests received no further consideration, but a hole was gnawed in a wooden door about 2.5 cm. thick. From there the birds got into a hayloft. In a corner of the 1.0 x 1.3 x 0.7 m. hayloft, three eggs were laid on the smooth floor boards. Probably both birds participated in incubation, because they were seen only for a brief while in the evening. The eggs were removed after six weeks of incubation, as all three were infertile.

In 1963, the first successful breeding was recorded. The macaws again used the hayloft as a nest. After an incubation period of about twenty-four days, one chick emerged from the clutch of the three eggs. After a nestling period of some three (?) months, the bird appeared in the aviary for the first time.

The well-known parrot fancier Wolfgang de Grahl, author of *Der Graupapagei* and *Papageien in Haus und Garten*, received four macaws of the nominate form in January 1975. After two of the birds turned out to be a pair, they were transferred to a flight 1.0 x 1.0 x 2.3 m. The cock could be distinguished from the hen by his broader, heavier head, the somewhat larger expanse of the bare facial area, and more massive shape. In March, four eggs were laid and incubated by the female. During the incubation period, the male always spent the night in the nest, and even during the day he often disappeared inside.

On April 1, a soft peeping could be heard from the breeding log. The nest was first inspected on April 10. The parents appeared extremely aggressive; the female even bit a finger severely and could be removed only with difficulty; in addition, both adults screamed without pause. In the nest were found one chick, covered with a very fine coat of down, and three eggs, two of which were infertile. The eggs were removed. The chick was well fed, as one could tell by its full crop. On the tenth day the eyes were still tightly closed; on the twentieth, they were open, and the dark feather sheaths could be seen glistening through the skin. At thirty days, the macaw weighed 150 g., and the first feathers could be seen on the wings and tail. At six weeks, the little fellow, which now weighed 180 g., was already well feathered. The beak was still horn colored at this time, and the iris was light brown. After the eighth week, the body weight was reduced to 160 g., a portent of impending flight. The beak now showed a more grayish color, and the feathers of the forecrown were a shiny black. The tail feathers were only about a third their natural length, and the wing linings showed only a small expanse of red. On the sixtieth day the young bird left the nest, accompanied by loud shrieks from the parent birds. Fourteen days later, the youngster was already eating sunflower seeds by itself. After eighty-five days, the beak was still lighter than that of an adult, and the bare facial patch was for a long time still not as extensive as that of the adult birds.

In Switzerland a successful breeding of the Red-shouldered Macaw occurred in 1978. A youngster was raised in an aviary that housed four individuals. Keeping Red-shouldered Macaws in a colony can be endorsed, although a flock must be provided with a large space to fly. If they are kept in pairs, optimal accommodations do not entail enclosures as large as those for the larger species. Unfortunately, Red-shouldered Macaws are very loud, and they often call shrilly without stopping for long periods of time. When keeping these birds in an outdoor flight, one must hope for tolerant neighbors.

Appendix

Museums. In the past two centuries, the natural-history museums have performed a service in the classification of birds. The principles of the system valid today were developed in these institutions. With a staff of workers spread over the entire world, birds were collected from all "corners" of the globe. Phylogeneticists and taxonomists measured, named, arranged, and described; craftsmen made skins, preparations, and illustrations. In the course of decades, thousands of pieces of information, like bits of a mosaic, were gathered together and systematized. Charles Darwin (1809-1882) with his theory of evolution created an essential foundation for the view of the world held by present-day natural science. At last, in 1931, James Lee Peters published the first volume of his 15-part *Check-list of Birds of the World,* in which the entire class of birds is encompassed in a single systematic presentation. The museums and their vast collections first and foremost made this species list possible. Every bird lover, bird keeper, bird breeder, and amateur ornithologist should not neglect to visit the multifarious collections of the natural-history museums in the course of his travels.

Following is a list of museums that display a part of the rich assortment of bird preparations, skins, skeletons, and eggs in their collections. One should consult with the museum administration about opportunities for visiting.

Australia
Melbourne: National Museum of Natural History, Geology, and Ethnology
Perth: Public Library, Museum, and Art Gallery of Western Australia
Sydney: Australian Museum
Sydney: MacLeay Museum of Natural History
Austria
Vienna: Naturhistorisches Museum
Belgium
Antwerp: Natuurwetenschappelijk Museum der Stadt Antwerpen

Brussels: Musée Royal d'Histoire Naturelle de Belgique
Czechoslovakia
Prague: National Museum
Denmark
Copenhagen: Zoological museum of the University of Copenhagen
France
Lyon: Muséum des Sciences Naturelles
Nancy: Muséé d'Histoire Naturelle
Paris: Muséum National d'Histoire Naturelle
Strasbourg: Musée Zoologique de l'Université et de la Ville
Toulouse: Muséum d'Histoire Naturelle et Jardin Zoologique
Federal Republic of Germany
Augsburg: Naturwissenschaftliches Museum
Bonn: Zoologischer Forschungs institut und Museum Alexander König
Braunschweig: Staatliches Naturhistorisches Museum
Bremen: Übersee-Museum
Coburg: Naturwissenschaftliches Museum der Coburger Landesstiftung
Darmstadt: Hessisches Landesmuseum
Erlangen: Zoologisches Institut der Friedrich-Alexander-Universität
Frankfurt: Forschungsinstitut und Naturmuseum Senckenberg
Göttingen: Zoologisches Institut der Universität Göttingen
Hamburg: Zoologisches Staatsinstitut und Zoológisches Museum
Hannover: Niedersächsisches Landesmuseum
Kassel: Städtisches Naturkundemuseum
Kiel: Zoologisches Institut und Museum der Universität Kiel
Munich: Zoologische Sammlung des Bayrischen Staates
Stuttgart: Staatliches Museum für Naturkunde
Tübingen: Zoologisches Institut der Universität Tübingen
Wilhelmshafen: Institut für Vogelforschung
German Democratic Republic
Berlin: Institut für Spezielle Zoologie und Zoologisches Museum der Humboldt-Universität

Dresden: Staatliches Museum für Tierkunde
Halle: Zoologisches Institut und Sammlung der Martin-Luther-Universtät
Leipzig: Zoologisches Institut der Karl-Marx-Universität
Leipzig: Naturkundliches Museum
Italy
Genoa: Museo Civico di Storia Naturale
Milan: Museo Civico di Storia Naturale
Naples: Museo Zoologico della Universita
Rome: Museo Civico di Zoologia
Turin: Museo di Zoologia
The Netherlands
Amsterdam: Zoologisches Museum der Universiteit Amsterdam
Leyden: Rijksmuseum van Natuurlijke Historie Leyden
Norway
Oslo: Zoological Museum of the University of Oslo
Sweden
Göteborg: Natural History Museum
Lund: Zoological Institute and Museum
Stockhlom: Royal Natural History Museum
Switzerland
Basel: Museum für Völkerkunde
Genf: Muséum d'Histoire Naturelle
Lansanne: Musée Zoologique de l'Université Lausanne
Neuchatel: Musée d'Histoire Naturelle
United Kingdom
Cambridge: University Museum of Zoology
Edinburgh: Royal Scottish Museum
Tring: British Museum (Natural History)
United States
Cambridge, MA: Museum of Comparative Zoology
Chicago: Chicago Academy of Sciences
Chicago: Chicago Natural History Museum
New York: American Museum of Natural History
San Diego: Natural History Museum
San Francisco: Pacific Museum of Ornithology
Washington: United States National Museum

Bird Parks and Zoos. Zoological gardens, with their broad palette of exotic animals, have always offered superior opportunities for observation and comparisons, not only to a wide public but to scientists as well.

It has been shown that the oldest zoological garden is the animal park of the Schönbrunn castle in Vienna. In 1752, the Emperor Francis I had this animal park built for his consort, the Empress Marie Theresa. Even then, in the eighteenth century, parrots were kept at Schönbrunn. The first zoological garden in Germany was the Stuttgart Menagerie, which was founded in 1812 but lasted only until 1816. The oldest German zoo still in existence is the Berlin Zoo, founded in 1841 and opened in 1844. Today this animal park can boast a collection richer in species than any other in Europe. For example, in 1978 there were 3071 birds, representing 713 species. But many other bird and animal parks, not only in Germany, also have a multifarious animal population on exhibit for visitors. For the bird fancier, and especially for the hookbill lover, a visit to one of the zoos or bird parks in the following list is recommended, although this listing can in no way be regarded as complete.

Austria
Vienna: Tiergarten Schönbrunn
Federal Republic of Germany
Berlin: Zoologischer Garten Berlin
Coesfeld: Vogelpark Müsterland
Detmold-Heiligenkirchen: Vogel- and Blumenpark Detmold-Heiligenkirchen
Duisburg: Zoo Duisburg
Frankfurt: Zoologischer Garten der Stadt Frankfurt
Geiselwind: Freizeit-Land (VPM-Park) Geiselwind
Gettorf: Tierpark Gettorf
Hamburg: Carl Hagenbeck's Tierpark
Hannover: Zoo Hannover
Irgenöd: Vogelpark Irgenöd
Metelen: Vogelpark Metelener Heide
Munich: Tierpark Hellabrunn
Steinen-Hofen (near Lörrach): Vogelpark Wiesental
Stuttgart: Zoologisch-Botanischer Garten Wilhelma
Thüle: Tierpark Worberg
Walsrode: Vogelpark Walsrode
Wuppertal-Eberfeld: Zoo Wuppertal
German Democratic Republic
Berlin: Tierpark Friedrichsfelde
Italy
Naples: Naples Zoo
The Netherlands
Amsterdam: Zoologischer Garten
Wasenaar: Tiergerten Wasenaar

Switzerland
Basel: Zoologischer Garten
Zürich: Zoologischer Garten
United Kingdom
Chester: Chester Zoo
London: London Zoo
Rode (near Bath): The Tropical Bird Gardens
Isle of Jersey: Jersey Wildlife Preservation Trust
United States
Chicago: Brookfield Zoo
Houston: Houston Zoo
Miami: Parrot Jungle
San Diego: San Diego Zoo
Tampa: Busch Gardens

For lovers of animals and parrot fanciers, animal and bird parks worth seeing will be found mainly in the larger cities (capitals) of Middle and South America, Africa, Southeast Asia, and Australia. Since many parrots are native to these regions, they are also well represented in these collections.

Associations and Specialist Periodicals. The bird fancy has flourished in the past years, and to a great extent this is manifest in the keeping of exotic birds. To be sure, this is not accomplished only by a love of birds in particular. Keeping an animal entails obligations and requirements that the responsible keeper must fulfill. This means that keepers and breeders of parrots are directed to continually exchange their experiences and information about their hobby. In almost every large town there is a group of interested persons and an association mainly concerned with keeping and breeding birds. Most meet once a month to discuss any current problems, whether they involve accommodations, feeding, breeding, or something else. Every society in the bird fancy will support newly interested persons both by word and deed.

A second opportunity for further information is offered by the specialist periodicals for bird fanciers, which as a rule appear monthly. Following are some German-language [and English-language] bird periodicals (and the abbreviations under which they are cited in the Bibliography).

Federal Republic of Germany
AZ-Nachrichten (AZ), "publication of the Central Exchange of German bird fanciers and breeders" (G. Wittenbrock, Vor der Elm 1, 2860 Osterholz-Scharmbeck, FRG).
Die Gefiederte Welt (Gef. Welt) (Verlag Eugen Ulmer, Wollgrasweg 41, 7000 Stuttgart 70, FRG).
Die Voliere (Verlag M. & H. Schaper, Grazer Str. 20, 3000 Hannover 81, FRG).
Geflügel Börse (Verlag Jürgens KG, Industriestr. 5, 8035 Gemering 1, FRG).
Kanarienfreund (Hanke Verlag GmbH, Postfach 1040, 7530 Pforzheim, FRG).
Trochilus (Biotrophic Verlag GmbH, Blochmatt 7, 7570 Baden-Baden, FRG).
ZZA—Zoologischer Zentral-Anzeiger (Zentralverband Zoologischer Fachgeschäfte Deutschlands e.V., 6057 Dietzenbach 1, Am Stadtbrunnen, FRG).
Switzerland
Gefiederter Freund (Gef. Freund) (D. Bischofberger, Mühlegasse 31, CH 6340 Baar/ZG, Switzerland)
United Kingdom
Avicultural Magazine, journal of the Avicultural Society (Windsor Forest Stud, Mill Ride, Ascot, Berkshire SL5 8LT, England).
Cage and Aviary Birds (Specialist and Professional Press, Surrey House, 1 Throwley Way, Sutton Surrey SM1 4QQ, UK).
Magazine of the Parrot Society (19a De Pary's Avenue, Bedford, England).
United States
The A.F.A. Watchbird, journal of the American Federation of Aviculture (Box 1568, Redondo Beach, CA 90278).
American Cage-Bird Magazine (1 Glamore Court, Smithtown, NY 11787).
Bird Talk (Box 3940, San Clememte, CA 92672).
Bird World (Box 70, North Hollywood, CA 91603).
Macaw Society Newsletter (229 West Basic Road, Henderson, NV 89105).
Parrot World, journal of the National Parrot Association (8 North Hoffman Lane, Hauppauge, NY 11788).

Bibliography

American Ornithologists' Union. 1983 (6th edn.). Check-list of North American birds. Lawrence, KS.

Atwood, T. 1791. *Hist. Id. Dominica, etc.*, p. 29.

Austin, O. L., Jr. 1961. *Birds of the world.* New York: Golden Press.

AZ-Nachrichten. *Vogelkrankheiten.* Sonderheft der AZ.

Bechstein. 1811. *Kurze Üb.*, p.64, pl. 1.

Bedford, 12th Duke of. 1954. *Parrots and parrot-like birds.* Fond du Lac, WI: All-Pets Books [Neptune, NJ: T.F.H. Publications]

Blecher, C., and Smooker, G. D. 1936. Birds of Trinidad and Tobago. *The Ibis* VI: 12-16.

Berndt, R., and Meise, W. 1962. *Naturgeschichte der Vögel.* Stuttgart: Franck'sche Verlagshandlung.

Bezzel, E. 1977. *Ornithologie.* Stuttgart: Verlag Eugen Ulmer.

Blake, E. R. 1953. *Birds of Mexico.* Chicago: University of Chicago Press.

Boetticher, H. v. 1962. *Papageien.* Wittenberg-Lutherstadt: A. Ziemsen-Verlag.

Bond, J. 1956. *Check-list of birds of the West Indies.* Philadelphia: Academy of Natural Sciences.

——. 1971 *Birds of the West Indies.* London: Collins.

Bouton, Pere. 1640. *Rel. de l'etab. d. Francais dep. 1635, en l'ile Martinique,* pp. 71-72.

Chapman, M. 1926. Macaws. *Bull. Amer. Mus. Nat. Hist.* LV: 253-256.

Chubb, Ch. 1916. *The Birds of British Guiana,* Vol. I. London: Bernard Quaritch.

Clarke. A. H. 1905. *Auk* 22: 345-348.

——. 1908. *Auk* 25: 309-311.

Clements, J. F. 1974. *Birds of the world: a check list.* New York: Two Continents.

Cordier, Ch. 1971. Über Lebensraum und Lebensweise der Felsenhähne. *Gef. Welt* 7/71: 133-136.

Darlington, P. J., Jr. 1931. Notes on the birds of Rio Frio, Magdalena, Colombia. *Bull. Mus. Comp. Zool. Harv.* 71: 349-421.

D'Aubenton le jeune. 1779. *Buffon's Planches Enluminées* 12.

Davis, L. I. 1972. *Birds of Mexico and Central America.* Austin and London: Univ. of Texas Press.

Dorst, J. 1972. *Die Vögel in ihrem Lebensraum.* Lausanne: Editions Recontre.

Dunning, J. S. 1982. *South American land birds.* Newton Square, PA: Harrowood Books.

Ebert, W. 1978. *Vogelkrankheiten.* Hannover: Schaper.

Edwards, E. P. 1968. *Finding birds in Mexico.* Sweet Briar, VA.

——. 1972. *A field guide to the birds of Mexico.* Sweet Briar, VA.

Edwards, E. P., and Loftin, H. 1971. *Finding birds in Panama.* Sweet Briar, VA.

Eisenmann, E., and Loftin, H. 1968. Birds of the Panama Canal Zone area. *Florida Naturalist* 41: 57-60.

ffrench, R. 1976. *A guide to the birds of Trinidad and Tobago.* Valley Forge, PA: Harrowood Books.

Fisher, J. N. S., and Vincent, J. 1969. *The red book: wildlife in danger.* London: Collins.

Forshaw, J. M. 1973. *Parrots of world.* Melbourne: Lansdowne Press [Neptune, NJ: T.F.H. Publications].

Freud, A. 1979. Lear's Macaw. *Magazine of the Parrot Society* XIII/2: 25-30.

Fuhs, K. and R. 1981. Geglückte Zucht eines Hellroten Ara (Arakanga). *AZ* 1/81: 14-15.

Gesner, C. 1669. *Vogelbuch.* Hannover: Schlütersche Verlagsanstalt und Druckerei, 1981.

Gosse, P. H. 1847. *The birds of Jamica.*

de Grahl, W. 1975. Erstzucht: *Ara nobilis nobilis* (Linnaeus). *Gef. Welt* 8/75: 141-143.

——. 1975. Papegeien-Idyll am Bodensee. *Gef. Welt* 10/75: 187-188.

——. 1977. *Papageien in Haus und Garten.* Stuttgart: Verlag Eugen Ulmer [In translation as *The Parrot Family.*]

Greenway, J. C., Jr. 1967. *Extinct and vanishing birds of the world.* New York: Dover Publications.

Grüning, E. 1981. Der erste in der Schweiz gezüchtete Marakana oder Rotrücken(Zwerg)ara? *Gef. Freund* 7/81: 171-173.

Gruson, E. S. 1976. *Checklist of the birds of the world.* London: Collins.

Günther, J. 1957. *Weiner Papageinbüchlein, nach Aquarellen von L. Brunner und L. Stoll.* Gütersloh: Bertelsmann Verlag.

Gyldenstolpe, N. 1945. *A contribution to the ornithology of northern Bolivia.* Stockholm: Almquist and Wiksells.

Haas, G. 1977. Ara-Zuchten im Wuppertaler Zoo. *AZ* 4/77: 111-114.

Haberlandt. 1928. Ein Besuch bei Blazers. *Vögel ferner Länder* II: 112-113.

Harnisch, W. 1975-76. *Mai's Auslandtaschenbuch, Nr. 28: Karibien und Mittelamerika.* Buchenhain: Verlag Volk und Heimat.

Haverschmidt, F. 1954. Evening flights of the Southern Everglade Kite and the Blue and Yellow Macaw in Surinam. *Wilson Bull.* 66: 264-265.

——. 1968. *Birds of Surinam.* Edinburgh: Oliver and Boyd.

Herklots, G. A. C. 1961. *The birds of Trinidad and Tobago.* London: Collins.

Herzog, M. 1978. Zuchterfolge bei den Zwergaras (Blaustirn Zwergaras) *Ara nobilis nobilis. Gef. Freund* 11/78: 277-279.

Hoppe, D. 1981. *Amazonen.* Stuttgart: Verlag Eugen Ulmar.

——. 1982. Nochmals: Caninde-Ara—Art oder Unterart? *Gef. Welt* 6/82: 188-189.

——. 1982. Über das Washingtoner Artenschutzübereinkommen. *Gef. Welt* 7/82: 222-225.

——. 1982. Zuchterfolge ohnegleichen beim Rotrückenara oder Maracana *(Ara maracana). Gef. Welt* 11/82: 347-348.

Howard, R., and Moore, A. 1980. *A complete checklist of the birds of the world.* New York: Oxford University Press.

Ingels, J., Parkes, K., and Farrand, J. 1981. The status of the macaw generally but incorrectly called *Ara caninda* (Wagler). *Gerfault* 71: 283-294.

Kirchhofer, E. 1973. Zucht des Ararauna. *Gef. Welt* 1/73: 1-3.

Kleiser, H. 1964. Brutversuche mit dem Zwergara. *Gef. Welt* 11/64: 206-207.

Köpcke, M. 1963. Probleme des Vogelzuges in Peru. *Proc. XIII Intern. Ornithol. Congr.*: 396-411.

Land, H. C. 1970. *Birds of Guatemala.* Wynnewood, PA: Livingston.

Laubmann, A. 1930. *Wissenschaftliche Ergebnisse der Deutschen Gran Chaco-Expedition, Vögel.* Stuttgart: Strecker und Schröder.

Le Vaillant. 1801. *Perr.* 1, p. 17, pl. 5.

Linn, H. 1978. Geglückte Zucht mit Gelbbrustara (Araruna). *AZ* 11/78: 372-374.

Bibliography

Loughlin, E. M. 1970. Field notes on the breeding and diet of some South American parrots. *Foreign Birds* 1970: 169-171.

Low, R. 1972. *The parrots of South America.* London: Gifford.

———. 1980. *Parrots, their care and breeding.* Poole, Dorset: Blandford Press.

Luther, D. 1970 *Die ausgestorbenen Vögel der Welt.* Wittenberg-Lutherstadt: A. Ziemsen-Verlag.

Maass, K. 1980. Zucht des Gelbnackenarara von K. Maass. *AZ* 1/80: 16.

Meier, E. 1978. Zucht des Gelbnacken(Zwerg)ara *(Ara auricollis). Gef. Freund* 9/78: 216-218.

Meyer de Schauensee, R. 1964 *The birds of Colombia.* Narbeth, PA: Livingston.

———. 1966. *The species of birds of South America.* Wynnewood, PA: Livingston.

———. 1970. *A guide to the birds of South America.* Wynnewood, PA: Livingston.

Mitchell, M. H. 1957. *Observations on birds of southeastern Brazil.* Toronto: Univ. of Toronto Press.

Monroe, B. L., Jr. 1968. *A distributional survey of the birds of Honduras.* AOU Ornithol. Monog. 7.

Naumberg, E. M. 1930. The birds of Mato Grosso: a report on the birds secured by the Roosevelt-Rondon Expedition. *Bull. Amer. Mus. Nat. Hist.* 60.

Navarette, Don de. 1838. Le gros perroquet de la Guadeloupe. *Rel. Quat. Voy. Christ.,* p. 425, pl. II.

Neunzig, K., and Russ, K. 1921. *Handbuch für Vogelliebhaber, -züchter und -händler.* Magdeburg: Creutzsche Verlagsbuchhandlung.

Niethammer, G. 1953. Zur Vogelwelt Boliviens. *Bonner Zool. Beiträge* 4: 195-303.

Olivares, A. 1969. *Aves de Cuncinamarca.* Univ. Nacional de Colombia: Dirrection de Divulgacion Cultural.

Olrog, C. Ch. 1959. *Las Aves Argentinas.* Buenos Aires: Instituto 'Miguel Lillo.'

———. 1968. *Las aves Sudamericanas.* Buenos Aires: Instituto 'Miquel Lillo.'

———. 1979. *Neuva lista de la avifauna Argentina.*

O'Neill, J. P. 1969. Distributional notes on the birds of Peru. *Occ. Pap. Mus. Zool. La. St. Univ.* 37: 1-11.

Peters, J. L. 1937. *Check-list of birds of the world.* Cambridge, MA: Harvard Univ. Press.

Peterson, R. T., and Chalif, E. L. 1973. *A field guide to Mexican birds.* Boston: Houghton Mifflin Co.

Phelps, W. H., and Phelps, W. H., Jr. 1958. *Lista de las aves de Venezuela con su distribucion.* Caracas: Editorial Sucre.

Pinto, O. M. de O. 1935. Aves de Bahia. *Rev. Mus. Paul.* 19.

———. 1950. Miscelanea orintologica (V). *Papéis Dep. Zool. S. Paulo* 9: 361-365.

Pinto, O. M. de O., and Camargo, E. A. de. 1948. Sôbre uma coleção de aves do Rio das Mortes (Estado de Mato Grosso). *Papéis Dep. Zool. S. Paulo* 8: 287-336.

Prestwich, A. A. 1963. *I name this parrot.* Edenbridge, Kent.

Reichenow, A. 1955. *Vogelbilder aus fernen Zonen—Papageien.* Pfungstadt, Helène.

Reinhard, R. 1982. Caninde-Ara—Art oder Unterart? *Gef. Welt* 4/82: 124.

Reynolds, M. 1977. *Cage and Aviary Birds* 10/77.

Ridgely, R. S. 1980. The current distribution and status of mainland neotropical parrots. In *Conservation of New World parrots,* ed. R. F. Pasquier. Washington: Smithsonian Inst. Press.

Robiller, F., and Trogisch, K. 1982. Ein Beitrag zum Verhalten des Hyazinthara. *Die Voliere* 6/82: 207-208.

de Rochefort. 1658. *Histoire Nat. & Mor. des Iles Antilles, &c.,* p. 154, Art. IX (Des Arras).

Roth, P. 1982. *Habitat-Aufteilung bei sympatrischen Papagein des südlichen Amazonasgebietes.* Zürich: Zentralstelle der Studentenschaft.

Rothschild, W. 1905. *Bull. Brit. Orn. Club* 16: 15.

———. 1907a. *Bull. IV Ornithol. Congr.:* 202.

———. 1907b. *Extinct Birds.* London: Hutchinson.

Ruschi, A. 1979. *Aves do Brasil.* São Paulo: Editoria Rios.

Russ, K. 1870. *Handbuch für Vogelliebhaber.*

———. 1891. *Die Papageien.* Magdeburg: Creutzsche Verlagsbuchhandlung.

———. 1898. *Die sprechenden Papageien.* Magdeburg: Creutzsche Verlagsbuchhandlung. [In translation as *The Speaking Parrots.*]

Sabel, K. 1961. *Vogelfutterpflanzen.* Pfungstadt: Helène.

Salvadori, T. 1906. Notes of parrots. *The Ibis,* Series 8, Vol. VI, p. 451.

Schönwetter, M. 1964. *Handbuch der Oologie.* Berlin: Akademie-Verlag.

Sclater, P. L. 1876. *Proc. Zool. Society London,* p. 225.

Sick, H. 1965. A fauna do cerrado. *Arq. Zool. Est. S. Paulo* 12: 71-93.

———. 1968. Vogelwanderungen im kontinentalen Südamerika. *Vogelwarte* 1968: 217-243.

———. 1979. Die Herkunft von Lear's Ara *(Anodorhynchus leari)* entdeckt! *Gef. Welt* 9/79: 161-162.

Snyder, D. E. 1966. *The birds of Guyana.* Salem: Peabody Museum.

Steinbacher, J. 1962. *Beiträge zur Kenntnis der Vögel von Paraguay.* Frankfurt: Abh. Senckenberg-Naturf. Ges.

———. 1968. *Weitere Beiträge über Vögel von Paraguay.* Frankfurt: Natur-Mus. u. Forsch. Inst. Senckenberg.

Stone, W., and Roberts, H. R. 1935. Zoological results of the Matto Grosso Expedition in Brazil in 1931, II: Birds. *Proc. Acad. Nat. Sci. Phila.* 86: 363-397.

Strassen, O. z. 1911. *Brehms Tierleben—Vögel—Dritter Band.* Leipzig and Vienna: Bibliographisches Institut.

Strunden, H. 1974. Papageien im Zoo von Rio de Janeiro. *Gef. Welt* 6/74: 104-105.

du Tertre, J. B. 1667. *Hist. gen. des Antilles,* Vol. II, p. 248.

Todd, W. E. C., and Carriker, M. A., Jr. The birds of the Santa Marta region of Colombia: a study in altitudinal distribution. *Ann. Carneg. Mus.* 14: 208.

Van Rossem, A. J., and Hachisuka, M. 1939. *Proc. Biol. Soc. Wash.* 52: 13.

Wagler, J. G. 1832. *Königl. Bayer. Akad. d. d. Wissensch.; Math.-Phys. Kl.* 1: 675.

Walters, M. 1980. *The complete birds of the world.* London: David & Charles; Neptune, NJ: T. F. H. Publications.

Wetmore, A. 1937. *Journ. Agr. Univ. Puerto Rico* 21: 12.

———. 1944. A collection of birds from Guanacaste, Costa Rica. *Proc. U. S. Natl. Mus.* 95: 25-80.

———. 1957. The birds of Isla Coiba, Panama. *Smithsonian Misc. Coll.* 134: 1-105.

———. 1968. *The birds of the Republic of Panama.* Washington: Smithsonian Inst. Press.

Wilking, G. 1981. Gelungene Zucht des Grüflügel oder Dunkelroten Arara *(Ara chloroptera). Gef. Welt* 3/81: 45-46.

Further reading on macaws from T. F. H. Publications:

Decoteau, A. E. 1982. *Handbook of macaws.*

Greene, W. T. 1884-87, 1979. *Parrots in captivity.*

Spiotta, L. 1979. *Macaws.*

Teitler, R. 1979. Taming and training macaws.

Indexes

References in boldface indicate illustrations.